The Hidden Power
And Other Papers on Mental Abilities

Thomas Troward

The Hidden Power and Other Papers on Mental Abilities
Copyright © 2014 by Bibliotech Press
All rights reserved.

Contact:
BibliotechPress@gmail.com

The present edition is a reproduction of 1936 publication of this work. Minor typographical errors may have been corrected without note, however, for an authentic reading experience the spelling, punctuation, and capitalization have been retained from the original text.

ISBN: 978-1-61895-142-7

CONTENTS

Chapter I	The Hidden Power	1
Chapter II	The Perversion of Truth	21
Chapter III	The "I Am"	29
Chapter IV	Affirmative Power	32
Chapter V	Submission	34
Chapter VI	Completeness	38
Chapter VII	The Principle of Guidance	42
Chapter VIII	Desire as the Motive Power	44
Chapter IX	Touching Lightly	48
Chapter X	Present Truth	51
Chapter XI	Yourself	53
Chapter XII	Religious Opinions	56
Chapter XIII	A Lesson from Browning	60
Chapter XIV	The Spirit of Opulence	63
Chapter XV	Beauty	66
Chapter XVI	Separation and Unity	69
Chapter XVII	Externalization	75

Chapter XVIII	Entering into the Spirit of It	78
Chapter XIX	The Bible and the New Thought	81
	I. The Son	81
	II. The Great Affirmation	88
	III. The Father	95
	IV. Conclusion	98
Chapter XX	Jachin and Boaz	102
Chapter XXI	Hephzibah	105
Chapter XXII	Mind and Hand	109
Chapter XXIII	The Central Control	111
Chapter XXIV	What is Higher Thought	113
Chapter XXV	Fragments	114

Chapter I

The Hidden Power

I

To realize fully how much of our present daily life consists in symbols is to find the answer to the old, old question, What is Truth? and in the degree in which we begin to recognize this we begin to approach Truth. The realization of Truth consists in the ability to translate symbols, whether natural or conventional, into their equivalents; and the root of all the errors of mankind consists in the inability to do this, and in maintaining that the symbol has nothing behind it. The great duty incumbent on all who have attained to this knowledge is to impress upon their fellow men that there is an *inner side* to things, and that until this *inner* side is known, the things themselves are not known.

There is an inner and an outer side to everything; and the quality of the superficial mind which causes it to fail in the attainment of Truth is its willingness to rest content with the outside only. So long as this is the case it is impossible for a man to grasp the import of his own relation to the universal, and it is this relation which constitutes all that is signified by the word "Truth." So long as a man fixes his attention only on the superficial it is impossible for him to make any progress in knowledge. He is denying that principle of "Growth" which is the root of all life, whether spiritual intellectual, or material, for he does not stop to reflect that all which he sees as the outer side of things can result only from some germinal principle hidden deep in the centre of their being.

Expansion from the centre by growth according to a necessary order of sequence, this is the Law of Life of which the whole universe is the outcome, alike in the one great solidarity of cosmic being, as in the separate individualities of its minutest organisms. This great principle is the key to the whole riddle of Life, upon whatever plane we contemplate it; and without this key the door from the outer to the inner side of things can never be opened. It is therefore the duty of all to whom this door has, at least in some measure, been opened, to Endeavour to acquaint others with the fact that there is an inner side to things, and that life becomes truer and fuller in proportion as we penetrate to it and make our estimates of all things according to what becomes visible from this interior point of view.

In the widest sense everything is a symbol of that which constitutes its inner being, and all Nature is a gallery of arcana revealing great truths to those who can decipher them. But there is a more precise sense in which our current life is based upon symbols in regard to the most important subjects that can occupy our thoughts: the symbols by which we strive to represent the nature and being of God, and the manner in which the life of man is related to the Divine life. The whole character of a man's life results from what he really believes on this subject: not his formal statement of belief in a particular creed, but what he realizes as the stage which his mind has actually attained in regard to it.

Has a man's mind only reached the point at which he thinks it is impossible to know anything about God, or to make any use of the knowledge if he had it? Then his whole interior world is in the condition of confusion, which must necessarily exist where no spirit of order has yet begun to move upon the chaos in which are, indeed, the elements of being, but all disordered and neutralizing one another. Has he advanced a step further, and realized that there is a ruling and an ordering power, but beyond this is ignorant of its nature? Then the unknown stands to him for the terrific, and, amid a tumult of fears and distresses that deprive him of all strength to advance, he spends his life in the Endeavour to propitiate this power as something naturally adverse to him, instead of knowing that it is the very centre of his own life and being.

And so on through every degree, from the lowest depths of ignorance to the greatest heights of intelligence, a man's life must always be the exact reflection of that particular stage which he has reached in the perception of the divine nature and of his own relation to it; and as we approach the full perception of Truth, so the life-principle within us expands, the old bonds and limitations which had no existence in reality fall off from us, and we enter into regions of light, liberty, and power, of which we had previously no conception. It is impossible, therefore, to overestimate the importance of being able to realize the symbol *for* a symbol, and being able to penetrate to the inner substance which it represents. Life itself is to be realized only by the conscious experience of its livingness in ourselves, and it is the Endeavour to translate these experiences into terms which shall suggest a corresponding idea to others that gives rise to all symbolism.

The nearer those we address have approached to the actual experience, the more transparent the symbol becomes; and the further they are from such experience the thicker is the veil; and our whole progress consists in the fuller and fuller translation of the symbols into clearer and clearer statements of that for which they stand. But the first step, without which all succeeding ones must remain impossible, is to convince people that symbols *are* symbols, and not the very Truth itself. And the difficulty consists in this, that if the symbolism is in any degree adequate it must, in some measure, represent the form of Truth, just as the modeling of a drapery suggests the form of the figure beneath. They have a certain consciousness that somehow they are in the presence of Truth; and this leads people to resent any removal of those folds of drapery which have hitherto conveyed this idea to their minds.

There is sufficient indication of the inner Truth in the outward form to afford an excuse for the timorous, and those who have not sufficient mental energy to think for themselves, to cry out that finality has already been attained, and that any further search into the matter must end in the destruction of Truth. But in raising such an outcry they betray their ignorance of the very nature of Truth, which is that it can never be destroyed: the very fact that Truth is Truth makes this impossible. And again they exhibit their ignorance of the first principle of Life—namely, the Law of Growth, which throughout the universe perpetually pushes forward into more and more vivid forms of expression, having expansion everywhere and finality nowhere.

Such ignorant objections need not, therefore, alarm us; and we should Endeavour to show those who make them that what they fear is the only natural order of the Divine Life, which is "over all, and through all, and in all." But we must do this gently, and not by forcibly thrusting upon them the object of their terror, and so repelling them from all study of the subject. We should Endeavour gradually to lead them to see that there is something interior to what they have hitherto held to be ultimate Truth, and to realize that the sensation of emptiness and dissatisfaction, which from time to time will persist in making itself felt in their hearts, is nothing else than the pressing forward of the spirit within to declare that inner side of things which alone can satisfactorily account for what we observe on the exterior, and without the knowledge of which we can never perceive the true nature of our inheritance in the Universal Life which is the Life Everlasting.

II

What, then, is this central principle which is at the root of all things? It is Life. But not life as we recognize it in particular forms of manifestation; it is something more interior and concentrated than that. It is that "unity of the spirit" which *is* unity, simply because it has not yet passed into diversity. Perhaps this is not an easy idea to grasp, but it is the root of all scientific conception of spirit; for without it there is no common principle to which we can refer the innumerable forms of manifestation that spirit assumes.

It is the conception of Life as the sum-total of all its undistributed powers, being as yet none of these in particular, but all of them in potentiality. This is, no doubt, a highly abstract idea, but it is essentially that of the centre from which growth takes place by expansion in every direction. This is that last residuum which defies all our powers of analysis. This is truly "the unknowable," not in the sense of the unthinkable but of the unanalysable. It is the subject of perception, not of knowledge, if by knowledge we mean that faculty which estimates the *relations* between things, because here we have passed beyond any questions of relations, and are face to face with the absolute.

This innermost of all is absolute Spirit. It is Life as yet not differentiated into any specific mode; it is the universal Life which pervades all things and is at the heart of all appearances.

To come into the knowledge of this is to come into the secret of power, and to enter into the secret place of Living Spirit. Is it illogical first to call this the unknowable, and then to speak of coming into the knowledge of it? Perhaps so; but no less a writer than St. Paul has set the example; for does he not speak of the final result of all searchings into the heights and depths and lengths and breadths of the inner side of things as being, to attain the knowledge of that Love which passeth knowledge. If he is thus boldly illogical in phrase, though not in fact, may we not also speak of knowing "the unknowable"? We may, for this knowledge is the root of all other knowledge.

The presence of this undifferentiated universal life-power is the final axiomatic fact to which all our analysis must ultimately conduct us. On whatever plane we make our analysis it must always abut upon pure essence, pure energy, pure being; that which knows itself and recognizes itself, but which cannot dissect itself because it is not built up of parts, but is ultimately integral: it is pure Unity. But analysis which does not lead to synthesis is merely destructive: it is the child wantonly pulling the flower to pieces and throwing away the fragments; not the botanist, also pulling the flower to pieces, but building up in his mind from those carefully studied fragments a vast synthesis of the constructive power of Nature, embracing the laws of the formation of all flower-forms. The value of analysis is to lead us to the original starting-point of that which we analyze, and so to teach us the laws by which its final form springs from this centre.

Knowing the law of its construction, we turn our analysis into a synthesis, and we thus gain a power of building up which must always be beyond the reach of those who regard "the unknowable" as one with "not-being."

This idea of the unknowable is the root of all materialism; and yet no scientific man, however materialistic his proclivities, treats the unanalyzable residuum thus when he meets it in the experiments of his laboratory. On the contrary, he makes this final unanalyzable fact the basis of his synthesis. He finds that in the last resort it is energy of some kind, whether as heat or as motion; but he does not throw up his scientific pursuits because he cannot analyze it further. He adopts the precisely opposite course, and realizes that the conservation of energy, its indestructibility, and the impossibility of adding to or detracting from the sum-total of energy in the world, is the one solid and unchanging fact on which alone the edifice of physical science can be built up.

He bases all his knowledge upon his knowledge of "the unknowable." And rightly so, for if he could analyze this energy into yet further factors, then the same problem of "the unknowable" would meet him still. All our progress consists in continually pushing the unknowable, in the sense of the unanalyzable residuum, a step further back; but that there should be no ultimate unanalyzable residuum anywhere is an inconceivable idea.

In thus realizing the undifferentiated unity of Living Spirit as the central fact of any system, whether the system of the entire universe or of a single organism, we are therefore following a strictly scientific method. We pursue our analysis until it necessarily leads us to this final fact, and then we accept this fact as the basis of our synthesis. The Science of Spirit is thus not one whit less scientific than the Science of Matter; and, moreover, it starts from the same initial fact, the fact of a living energy which defies definition or explanation, wherever we find it; but it differs from the science of matter in that it contemplates this energy under an aspect of responsive intelligence which does not fall within the scope of physical science, as such. The Science of Spirit and the Science of Matter are not opposed. They are complementaries, and neither is fully comprehensible without some knowledge of the other; and, being really but two portions of one whole, they insensibly shade off into each other in a border-land where no arbitrary line can be drawn between them. Science studied in a truly scientific spirit, following out its own deductions unflinchingly to their legitimate conclusions, will always reveal the twofold aspect of things, the inner and the outer; and it is only a truncated and maimed science that refuses to recognize both.

The study of the material world is not Materialism, if it be allowed to progress to its legitimate issue. Materialism is that limited view of the universe which will not admit the existence of anything but mechanical effects of mechanical causes, and a system which recognizes no higher power than the physical forces of nature must logically result in having no higher ultimate appeal than to physical force or to fraud as its alternative. I speak, of course, of the tendency of the system, not of the morality of individuals, who are often very far in advance of the systems they profess. But as we would avoid the propagation of a mode of thought whose effects history shows only too plainly, whether in the Italy of the Borgias, or the France of the First Revolution, or the Commune of the Franco-Prussian War, we should set ourselves to study that inner and spiritual aspect of things which is the basis of a system whose logical results are truth and love instead of perfidy and violence.

Some of us, doubtless, have often wondered why the Heavenly Jerusalem is described in the Book of Revelations as a cube; "the length and the breadth and the height of it are equal." This is because the cube is the figure of perfect stability, and thus represents Truth, which can never be overthrown. Turn it on what side you will, it still remains the perfect cube, always standing upright; you cannot upset it. This figure, then, represents the manifestation in concrete solidity of that central life-giving energy, which is not itself any one plane but generates all planes, the planes of the above and of the below and of all four sides. But it is at the same time a city, a place of habitation; and this is because that which is "the within" is Living Spirit, which has its dwelling there.

As one plane of the cube implies all the other planes and also "the within," so any plane of manifestation implies the others and also that "within" which generates them all. Now, if we would make any progress in the spiritual side of science—and *every* department of science has its spiritual side—we must always keep our minds fixed upon this "innermost within" which contains the potential of all outward manifestation, the "fourth dimension" which generates the cube; and our common forms of speech show how intuitively we do this. We speak of the spirit in which an act is done, of entering into the spirit of a game, of the spirit of the time, and so on. Everywhere our intuition points out the spirit as the true essence of things; and it is only when we commence arguing about them from without, instead of from within, that our true perception of their nature is lost.

The scientific study of spirit consists in following up intelligently and according to definite method the same principle that now only flashes upon us at intervals fitfully and vaguely. When we once realize that this universal and unlimited power of spirit is at the root of all things and of ourselves also, then we have obtained the key to the whole position; and, however far we may carry our studies in spiritual science, we shall nowhere find anything else but particular developments of this one universal principle. "The Kingdom of Heaven is *within* you."

III

I have laid stress on the fact that the "innermost within" of all things is living Spirit, and that the Science of Spirit is distinguished from the Science of Matter in that it contemplates Energy under an aspect of responsive intelligence which does not fall within the scope of physical science, as such. These are the two great points to lay hold of if we would retain a clear idea of Spiritual Science, and not be misled by arguments drawn from the physical side of Science only—the livingness of the originating principle which is at the heart of all things, and its intelligent and responsive nature. Its livingness is patent to our observation, at any rate from the point where we recognize it in the vegetable kingdom; but its intelligence and responsiveness are not, perhaps, at once so obvious. Nevertheless, a little thought will soon lead us to recognize this also.

No one can deny that there is an intelligent order throughout all nature, for it requires the highest intelligence of our most highly-trained minds to follow the steps of this universal intelligence which is always in advance of them. The more deeply we investigate the world we live in, the more clear it must become to us that all our science is the translation into words or numerical symbols of that order which already exists. If the clear statement of this existing order is the highest that the human intellect can reach, this surely argues a corresponding intelligence in the power which gives rise to this great sequence of order and interrelation, so as to constitute one harmonious whole. Now, unless we fall back on the idea of a workman working upon material external to himself—in which case we have to explain the phenomenon of the workman—the only conception we can form of this power is that it is the Living Spirit inherent in the heart of every atom, giving it outward form and definition, and becoming in it those intrinsic polarities which constitute its characteristic nature.

There is no random work here. Every attraction and repulsion acts with its proper force collecting the atoms into molecules, the molecules into tissues, the tissues into organs, and the organs into individuals. At each stage of the progress we get the sum of the intelligent forces which operate in the constituent parts, *plus* a higher degree of intelligence which we may regard as the collective intelligence superior to that of the mere sum-total of the parts, something which belongs to the individual *as a whole*, and not to the parts as such. These are facts which can be amply proved from physical science; and they also supply a great law in spiritual science, which is that in any collective body the intelligence of the whole is superior to that of the sum of the parts.

Spirit is at the root of all things, and thoughtful observation shows that its operation is guided by unfailing intelligence which adapts means to ends, and harmonizes the entire universe of manifested being in those wonderful ways which physical science renders clearer every day; and this intelligence must be in the generating spirit itself, because there is no other source from which it could proceed. On these grounds, therefore, we may distinctly affirm that Spirit is intelligent, and that whatever it does is done by the intelligent adaptation of means to ends.

But Spirit is also responsive. And here we have to fall back upon the law above stated, that the mere sum of the intelligence of Spirit in lower degrees of manifestation is not equal to the intelligence of the complex *whole*, as a whole. This is a radical law which we cannot impress upon our minds too deeply. The degree of spiritual intelligence is marked by the wholeness of the organism through which it finds expression; and therefore the more highly organized being has a degree of spirit which is superior to, and consequently capable of exercising control over, all lower or less fully-integrated degrees of spirit; and this being so, we can now begin to see why the spirit that is the "innermost within" of all things is responsive as well as intelligent.

Being intelligent, it *knows*, and spirit being ultimately all there is, that which it knows is itself. Hence it is that power which recognizes itself; and accordingly the lower powers of it recognize its higher powers, and by the law of attraction they are bound to respond to the higher degrees of themselves. On this general principle, therefore, spirit, under whatever exterior revealed, is necessarily intelligent and responsive. But intelligence and responsiveness imply personality; and we may therefore now advance a step further and argue that *all* spirit contains the elements of personality, even though, in any particular instance, it may not yet be expressed as that individual personality which we find in ourselves.

In short, spirit is always personal in its nature, even when it has not yet attained to that degree of synthesis which is sufficient to render it personal in manifestation. In ourselves the synthesis has proceeded far enough to reach that degree, and therefore we recognize ourselves as the manifestation of personality. The human kingdom is the kingdom of the manifestation of that personality, which is of the essence of spiritual substance on every plane. Or, to put the whole argument in a simpler form, we may say that our own personality must necessarily have had its origin in that which is personal, on the principle that you cannot get more out of a bag than it contains.

In ourselves, therefore, we find that more perfect synthesis of the spirit into manifested personality which is wanting in the lower kingdoms of nature, and, accordingly, since spirit is necessarily that which knows itself and must, therefore, recognize its own degrees in its various modes, the spirit in all degrees below that of human personality is bound to respond to itself in that superior degree which constitutes human individuality; and this is the basis of the power of human thought to externalize itself in infinite forms of its own ordering.

But if the subordination of the lower degrees of spirit to the higher is one of the fundamental laws which lie at the bottom of the creative power of thought, there is another equally fundamental law which places a salutary restraint upon the abuse of that power. It is the law that we can command the powers of the universal for our own purposes only in proportion as we first realize and obey their generic character. We can employ water for any purpose which does not require it to run up-hill, and we can utilize electricity for any purpose that does not require it to pass from a lower to a higher potential.

So with that universal power which we call the Spirit. It has an inherent generic character with which we must comply if we would employ it for our specific purposes, and this character is summed up in the one word "goodness." The Spirit is Life, hence its generic tendency must always be lifeward or to the increase of the livingness of every individual. And since it is universal it can have no particular interests to serve, and therefore its action must always be equally for the benefit of all. This is the generic character of spirit; and just as water, or electricity, or any other of the physical forces of the universe, will not work contrary to their generic character, so Spirit will not work contrary to its generic character.

The inference is obvious. If we would use Spirit we must follow the law of the Spirit which is "Goodness." This is the only limitation. If our originating intention is good, we may employ the spiritual power for what purpose we will. And how is "goodness" to be defined? Simply by the child's definition that what is bad is not good, and that what is good is not bad; we all know the difference between bad and good instinctively. If we will conform to this principle of obedience to the generic law of the Spirit, all that remains is for us to study the law of the proportion which exists between the more and less fully integrated modes of Spirit, and then bring our knowledge to bear with determination.

IV

The law of spirit, to which our investigation has now led us, is of the very widest scope. We have followed it up from the conception of the intelligence of spirit, subsisting in the initial atoms, to the aggregation of this intelligence as the conscious identity of the individual. But there is no reason why this law should cease to operate at this point, or at any point short of the whole. The test of the soundness of any principle is that it can operate as effectively on a large scale as on a small one, that though the nature of its field is determined by the nature of the principle itself, the extent of its field is unlimited. If, therefore, we continue to follow up the law we have been considering, it leads us to the conception of a unit of intelligence as far superior to that of the individual man as the unity of his individual intelligence is superior to that of the intelligence of any single atom of his body; and thus we may conceive of a collective individuality representing the spiritual character of any aggregate of men, the inhabitants of a city, a district, a country, or of the entire world.

Nor need the process stop here. On the same principle there would be a superior collective individuality for the humanity of the entire solar system, and finally we reach the conception of a supreme intelligence bringing together in itself the collective individualities of all the systems in the universe. This is by no means a merely fanciful notion. We find it as the law by which our own conscious individuality is constituted; and we find the analogous principle working universally on the physical plane. It is known to physical science as the "law of inverse squares," by which the forces of reciprocal attraction or repulsion, as the case may be, are not merely equivalent to the sum of the forces emitted by the two bodies concerned, but are equivalent to these two forces multiplied together and divided by the square of the distance between them, so that the resultant power continually rises in a rapidly-increasing ratio as the two reciprocally exciting bodies approach one another.

Since this law is so universal throughout physical nature, the doctrine of continuity affords every ground for supposing that its analogue holds good in respect of spiritual nature. We must never lose sight of the old-world saying that "a truth on one plane is a truth on all." If a principle exists at all it exists universally. We must not allow ourselves to be misled by appearances; we must remember that the perceptible results of the working of any principle consist of two factors—the principle itself or the active factor, and the subject-matter on which it acts or the passive factor; and that while the former is invariable, the latter is variable, and that the operation of the same invariable upon different variables must necessarily produce a variety of results. This at once becomes evident if we state it mathematically; for example, a, b or c, multiplied by x give respectively the results ax, bx, cx, which differ materially from one another, though the factor x always remains the same.

This law of the generation of power by attraction applies on the spiritual as well as on the physical plane, and acts with the same mathematical precision on both; and thus the human individuality consists, not in the mere aggregation of its parts, whether spiritual or corporeal, but in the *unity* of power resulting from the intimate association into which those parts enter with one another, which unity, according to this law of the generation of power by attraction, is infinitely superior, both in intelligence and power, to any less fully integrated mode of spirit. Thus a natural principle, common alike to physical and spiritual law, fully accounts for all claims that have ever been made for the creative power of our thought over all things that come within the circle of our own particular life. Thus it is that each man is the centre of his own universe, and has the power, by directing his own thought, to control all things therein.

But, as I have said above, there is no reason why this principle should not be recognized as expanding from the individual until it embraces the entire universe. Each man, as the centre of his own world, is himself centered in a higher system in which he is only one of innumerable similar atoms, and this system again in a higher until we reach the supreme centre of all things; intelligence and power increase from centre to centre in a ratio rising with inconceivable rapidity, according to the law we are now investigating, until they culminate in illimitable intelligence and power commensurate with All-Being.

Now we have seen that the relation of man to the lower modes of spirit is that of superiority and command, but what is his relation to these higher modes? In any harmoniously constituted system the relation of the part to the whole never interferes with the free operation of the part in the performance of its own functions; but, on the contrary, it is precisely by means of this relation that each part is maintained in a position to discharge all functions for which it is fitted. Thus, then, the subordination of the individual man to the supreme mind, so far from curtailing his liberty, is the very condition which makes liberty possible, or even life itself. The generic movement of the whole necessarily carries the part along with it; and so long as the part allows itself thus to be carried onwards there will be no hindrance to its free working in any direction for which it is fitted by its own individuality. This truth was set forth in the old Hindu religion as the Car of Jaggarnath—an ideal car only, which later ages degraded into a terribly material symbol. "Jaggarnath" means "Lord of the Universe," and thus signifies the Universal Mind. This, by the law of Being, must always move forward regardless of any attempts of individuals to restrain it. Those who mount upon its car move onward with it to endlessly advancing evolution, while those who seek to oppose it must be crushed beneath its wheels, for it is no respecter of persons.

If, therefore, we would employ the universal law of spirit to control our own little individual worlds, we must also recognize it in respect to the supreme centre round which we ourselves revolve. But not in the old way of supposing that this centre is a capricious Individuality external to ourselves, which can be propitiated or cajoled into giving the good which he is not good enough to give of his own proper motion. So long as we retain this infantile idea we have not come into the liberty which results from the knowledge of the certainty of Law. Supreme Mind is Supreme Law, and can be calculated upon with the same accuracy as when manifested in any of the particular laws of the physical world; and the result of studying, understanding and obeying this Supreme Law is that we thereby acquire the power to *use* it. Nor need we fear it with the old fear which comes from ignorance, for we can rely with confidence upon the proposition that the whole can have no interest adverse to the parts of which it is composed; and conversely that the part can have no interest adverse to the whole.

Our ignorance of our relation to the whole may make us appear to have separate interests, but a truer knowledge must always show such an idea to be mistaken. For this reason, therefore, the same responsiveness of spirit which manifests itself as obedience to our wishes, when we look to those degrees of spirit which are lower than her own individuality, must manifest itself as a necessary inflowing of intelligence and power when we look to the infinity of spirit, of which our individuality is a singular expression, because in so looking upwards we are looking for the higher degrees of *ourself*.

The increased vitality of the parts means the increased vitality of the whole, and since it is impossible to conceive of spirit otherwise than as a continually expanding principle of Life, the demand for such increased vitality must, by the inherent nature of spirit, be met by a corresponding supply of continually growing intelligence and power. Thus, by a natural law, the demand creates the supply, and this supply may be freely applied to any and every subject-matter that commends itself to us. There is no limit to the supply of this energy other than what we ourselves put to it by our thought; nor is there any limit to the purposes we may make it serve other than the one grand Law of Order, which says that good things used for wrong purposes become evil. The consideration of the intelligent and responsive nature of spirit shows that there can be no limitations but these. The one is a limitation inherent in spirit itself, and the other is a limitation which has no root except in our own ignorance.

It is true that to maintain our healthy action within the circle of our own individual world we must continually move forward with the movement of the larger whole of which we form a part. But this does not imply any restriction of our liberty to make the fullest use of our lives in accordance with those universal principles of life upon which they are founded; for there is not one law for the part and another for the whole, but the same law of Being permeates both alike. In proportion, therefore, as we realize the true law of our own individuality we shall find that it is one with the law of progress for the race. The collective individuality of mankind is only the reproduction on a larger scale of the personal individuality; and whatever action truly develops the inherent powers of the individual must necessarily be in line with that forward march of the universal mind which is the evolution of humanity as a whole.

Selfishness is a narrow view of our own nature which loses sight of our place in relation to the whole, not perceiving that it is from this very relation that our life is drawn. It is ignorance of our own possibilities and consequent limitation of our own powers. If, therefore, the evidence of harmonious correlation throughout the physical world leads irresistibly to the inference of intelligent spirit as the innermost within of all things, we must recognize ourselves also as individual manifestations of the same spirit which expresses itself throughout the universe as that power of intelligent responsiveness which is Love.

V

Thus we find ourselves to be a necessary and integral part of the Infinite Harmony of All-Being; not merely recognizing this great truth as a vague intuition, but as the logical and unavoidable result of the universal Life-principle which permeates all Nature. We find our intuition was true because we have discovered the law which gave rise to it; and now intuition and investigation both unite in telling us of our own individual place in the great scheme of things. Even the most advanced among us have, as yet, little more than the faintest adumbration of what this place is. It is the place of *power*. Towards those higher modes of spirit which we speak of as "the universal," the law of man's inmost nature makes him as a lens, drawing into the focus of his own individuality all that he will of light and power in streams of inexhaustible supply; and towards the lower modes of spirit, which form for each one the sphere of his own particular world, man thus becomes the directive centre of energy and order.

Can we conceive of any position containing greater possibilities than these? The circle of this vital influence may expand as the individual grows into the wider contemplation of his unity with Infinite Being; but any more comprehensive law of relationship it would be impossible to formulate. Emerson has rightly said that a little algebra will often do far more towards clearing our ideas than a large amount of poetic simile. Algebraically it is a self-evident proposition that any difference between various powers of x disappears when they are compared with x multiplied into itself to infinity, because there can be no ratio between any determinate power, however high, and the infinite; and thus the relation between the individual and All-Being must always remain the same.

But this in no way interferes with the law of growth, by which the individual rises to higher and higher powers of his own individuality. The unchangeableness of the relation between all determinate powers of x and infinity does not affect the relations of the different powers of x between themselves; but rather the fact that the multiplication of x into itself to infinity is mentally conceivable is the very proof that there is no limit to the extent to which it is possible to raise x in its determinate powers.

I trust unmathematical readers will pardon my using this method of statement for the benefit of others to whom it will carry conviction. A relation once clearly grasped in its mathematical aspect becomes thenceforth one of the unalterable truths of the universe, no longer a thing to be argued about, but an axiom which may be assumed as the foundation on which to build up the edifice of further knowledge. But, laying aside mathematical formula, we may say that because the Infinite is infinite there can be no limit to the extent to which the vital principle of growth may draw upon it, and therefore there is no limit to the expansion of the individual's powers. Because we are *what* we are, we may *become* what we will.

The Kabbalists tell us of "the lost word," the word of power which mankind has lost. To him who discovers this word all things are possible. Is this mirific word really lost? Yes, and No. It is the open secret of the universe, and the Bible gives us the key to it. It tells us, "The Word is nigh thee, even in thy mouth and in thy heart." It is the most familiar of all words, the word which in our heart we realize as the centre of our conscious being, and which is in our mouth a hundred times a day. It is the word "I AM." Because I am what I am, I may be what I will to be. My individuality is one of the modes in which the Infinite expresses itself, and therefore I am myself that very power which I find to be the innermost within of all things.

To me, thus realizing the great unity of all Spirit, the infinite is not the indefinite, for I see it to be the infinite of *Myself*. It is the very same I AM that I am; and this not by any act of uncertain favor, but by the law of polarity which is the basis of all Nature. The law of polarity is that law according to which everything attains completion by manifesting itself in the opposite direction to that from which it started. It is the simple law by which there can be no inside without an outside, nor one end of a stick without an opposite end.

Life is motion, and all motion is the appearance of energy at another point, and, where any work has been done, under another form than that in which it originated; but wherever it reappears, and in whatever new form, the vivifying energy is still the same. This is nothing else than the scientific doctrine of the conservation of energy, and it is upon this well-recognized principle that our perception of ourselves as integral portions of the great universal power is based.

We do well to pay heed to the sayings of the great teachers who have taught that all power is in the "I AM," and to accept this teaching by faith in their bare authority rather than not accept it at all; but the more excellent way is to know *why* they taught thus, and to realize for ourselves this first great law which all the master-minds have realized throughout the ages. It is indeed true that the "lost word" is the one most familiar to us, ever in our hearts and on our lips. We have lost, not the word, but the realization of its power. And as the infinite depths of meaning which the words I AM carry with them open out to us, we begin to realize the stupendous truth that we are ourselves the very power which we seek.

It is the polarization of Spirit from the universal into the particular, carrying with it all its inherent powers, just as the smallest flame has all the qualities of fire. The I AM in the individual is none other than the I AM in the universal. It is the same Power working in the smaller sphere of which the individual is the centre. This is the great truth which the ancients set forth under the figure of the Macrocosm and the Microcosm, the lesser I AM reproducing the precise image of the greater, and of which the Bible tells us when it speaks of man as the image of God.

Now the immense practical importance of this principle is that it affords the key to the great law that "as a man thinks so he is." We are often asked why this should be, and the answer may be stated as follows: We know by personal experience that we realize our own livingness in two ways, by our power to act and our susceptibility to feel; and when we consider Spirit in the absolute we can only conceive of it as these two modes of livingness carried to infinity. This, therefore, means infinite susceptibility. There can be no question as to the degree of sensitiveness, for Spirit *is* sensitiveness, and is thus infinitely plastic to the slightest touch that is brought to bear upon it; and hence every thought we formulate sends its vibrating currents out into the infinite of Spirit, producing there currents of like quality but of far vaster power.

But Spirit in the Infinite is the Creative Power of the universe, and the impact of our thought upon it thus sets in motion a veritable creative force. And if this law holds good of one thought it holds good of all, and hence we are continually creating for ourselves a world of surroundings which accurately reproduces the complexion of our own thoughts. Persistent thoughts will naturally produce a greater external effect than casual ones not centered upon any particular object. Scattered thoughts which recognize no principle of unity will fail to reproduce any principle of unity. The thought that we are weak and have no power over circumstances results in inability to control circumstances, and the thought of power produces power.

At every moment we are dealing with an infinitely sensitive medium which stirs creative energies that give form to the slightest of our thought-vibrations. This power is inherent in us because of our spiritual nature, and we cannot divest ourselves of it. It is our truly tremendous heritage because it is a power which, if not intelligently brought into lines of orderly activity, will spend its uncontrolled forces in devastating energy. If it is not used to build up, it will destroy. And there is nothing exceptional in this: it is merely the reappearance on the plane of the universal and undifferentiated of the same principle that pervades all the forces of Nature. Which of these is not destructive unless drawn off into some definite direction? Accumulated steam, accumulated electricity, accumulated water, will at length burst forth, carrying destruction all around; but, drawn off through suitable channels, they become sources of constructive power, inexhaustible as Nature itself.

And here let me pause to draw attention to this idea of accumulation. The greater the accumulation of energy, the greater the danger if it be not directed into a proper order, and the greater the power if it be. Fortunately for mankind the physical forces, such as electricity, do not usually subsist in a highly concentrated form. Occasionally circumstances concur to produce such concentration, but as a rule the elements of power are more or less equally dispersed. Similarly, for the mass of mankind, this spiritual power has not yet reached a very high degree of concentration. Every mind, it is true, must be in some measure a centre of concentration, for otherwise it would have no conscious individuality; but the power of the individualized mind rapidly rises as it recognizes its unity with the Infinite life, and its thought-currents, whether well or ill directed, then assume a proportionately great significance.

Hence the ill effects of wrongly directed thought are in some degree mitigated in the great mass of mankind, and many causes are in operation to give a right direction to their thoughts, though the thinkers themselves are ignorant of what thought-power is. To give a right direction to the thoughts of ignorant thinkers is the purpose of much religious teaching, which these uninstructed ones must accept by faith in bare authority because they are unable to realize its true import. But notwithstanding the aids thus afforded to mankind, the general stream of unregulated thought cannot but have an adverse tendency, and hence the great object to which the instructed mind directs its power is to free itself from the entanglements of disordered thought, and to help others to do the same. To escape from this entanglement is to attain perfect Liberty, which is perfect Power.

VI

The entanglement from which we need to escape has its origin in the very same principle which gives rise to liberty and power. It is the same principle applied under inverted conditions. And here I would draw particular attention to the law that any sequence followed out in an inverted order must produce an inverted result, for this goes a long way to explain many of the problems of life. The physical world affords endless examples of the working of "inversion." In the dynamo the sequence commences with mechanical force which is ultimately transformed into the subtler power of electricity; but invert this order, commence by generating electricity, and it becomes converted into mechanical force, as in the motor. In the one order the rotation of a wheel produces electricity, and in the opposite order electricity produces the rotation of a wheel. Or to exhibit the same principle in the simplest arithmetical form, if $10 \div 2 = 5$ then $10 \div 5 = 2$. "Inversion" is a factor of the greatest magnitude and has to be reckoned with; but I must content myself here with only indicating the general principle that the same power is capable of producing diametrically opposite effects if it be applied under opposite conditions, a truth which the so-called "magicians" of the middle ages expressed by two triangles placed inversely to one another. We are apt to fall into the mistake of supposing that results of opposite character require powers of opposite character to produce them, and our conceptions of things in general become much simplified when we recognize that this is not the case, but that the same power will produce opposite results as it starts from opposite poles.

Accordingly the inverted application of the same principle which gives rise to liberty and power constitutes the entanglement from which we need to be delivered before power and liberty can be attained, and this principle is expressed in the law that "as a man thinks so he is." This is the basic law of the human mind. It is Descartes' "*cogito, ergo sum*." If we trace consciousness to its seat we find that it is purely subjective. Our external senses would cease to exist were it not for the subjective consciousness which perceives what they communicate to it.

The idea conveyed to the subjective consciousness may be false, but until some truer idea is more forcibly impressed in its stead it remains a substantial reality to the mind which gives it objective existence. I have seen a man speak to the stump of a tree which in the moonlight looked like a person standing in a garden, and repeatedly ask its name and what it wanted; and so far as the speaker's conception was concerned the garden contained a living man who refused to answer. Thus every mind lives in a world to which its own perceptions give objective reality. Its perceptions may be erroneous, but they nevertheless constitute the very reality of life for the mind that gives form to them. No other life than the life we lead in our own mind is possible; and hence the advance of the whole race depends on substituting the ideas of good, of liberty, and of order for their opposites. And this can be done only by giving some sufficient reason for accepting the new idea in place of the old. For each one of us our beliefs constitute our facts, and these beliefs can be changed only by discovering some ground for a different belief.

This is briefly the rationale of the maxim that "as a man thinks so he is"; and from the working of this principle all the issues of life proceed. Now man's first perception of the law of cause and effect in relation to his own conduct is that the result always partakes of the quality of the cause; and since his argument is drawn from external observation only, he regards external acts as the only causes he can effectively set in operation. Hence when he attains sufficient moral enlightenment to realize that many of his acts have been such as to merit retribution he fears retribution as their proper result. Then by reason of the law that "thoughts are things," the evils which he fears take form and plunge him into adverse circumstances, which again prompt him into further wrong acts, and from these come a fresh crop of fears which in their turn become externalized into fresh evils, and thus arises a circulus from which there is no escape so long as the man recognizes nothing but his external acts as a causative power in the world of his surroundings.

This is the Law of Works, the Circle of Karma, the Wheel of Fate, from which there appears to be no escape, because the complete fulfillment of the law of our moral nature to-day is only sufficient for to-day and leaves no surplus to compensate the failure of yesterday. This is the necessary law of things as they appear from external observation only; and, so long as this conception remains, the law of each man's subjective consciousness makes it a reality for him. What is needed, therefore, is to establish the conception that external acts are NOT the only causative power, but that there is another law of causation, namely, that of pure Thought. This is the Law of Faith, the Law of Liberty; for it introduces us to a power which is able to inaugurate a new sequence of causation not related to any past actions.

But this change of mental attitude cannot be brought about till we have laid hold of some fact which is sufficient to afford a reason for the change. We require some solid ground for our belief in this higher law. Ultimately we find this ground in the great Truth of the eternal relation between spirit in the universal and in the particular. When we realize that substantially there is nothing else *but* spirit, and that we ourselves are reproductions in individuality of the Intelligence and Love which rule the universe, we have reached the firm standing ground where we find that we can send forth our Thought to produce any effect we will. We have passed beyond the idea of two opposites requiring reconciliation, into that of a duality in which there is no other opposition than that of the inner and the outer of the same unity, the polarity which is inherent in all Being, and we then realize that in virtue of this unity our Thought is possessed of illimitable creative power, and that it is free to range where it will, and is by no means bound down to accept as inevitable the consequences which, if unchecked by renovated thought, would flow from our past actions.

In its own independent creative power the mind has found the way out of the fatal circle in which its previous ignorance of the highest law had imprisoned it. The Unity of the Spirit is found to result in perfect Liberty; the old sequence of Karma has been cut off, and a new and higher order has been introduced. In the old order the line of thought received its quality from the quality of the actions, and since they always fell short of perfection, the development of a higher thought-power from this root was impossible. This is the order in which everything is seen from *without*. It is an inverted order. But in the true order everything is seen from *within*.

It is the thought which determines the quality of the action, and not *vice versa*, and since thought is free, it is at liberty to direct itself to the highest principles, which thus spontaneously reproduce themselves in the outward acts, so that both thoughts and actions are brought into harmony with the great eternal laws and become one in purpose with the Universal Mind. The man realizes that he is no longer bound by the consequences of his former deeds, done in the time of his ignorance, in fact, that he never was bound by them except so far as he himself gave them this power by false conceptions of the truth; and thus recognizing himself for what he really is—the expression of the Infinite Spirit in individual personality—he finds that he is free, that he is a "partaker of Divine nature," not losing his identity, but becoming more and more fully himself with an ever-expanding perfection, following out a line of evolution whose possibilities are inexhaustible.

But there is not in all men this knowledge. For the most part they still look upon God as an individual Being external to themselves, and what the more instructed man sees to be unity of mind and identity of nature appear to the less advanced to be an external reconciliation between opposing personalities. Hence the whole range of conceptions which may be described as the Messianic Idea. This idea is not, as some seem to suppose, a misconception of the truth of Being. On the contrary, when rightly understood it will be found to imply the very widest grasp of that truth; and it is from the platform of this supreme knowledge alone that an idea so comprehensive in its adaptation to every class of mind could have been evolved. It is the translation of the relations arising from the deepest laws of Being into terms which can be realized even by the most unlearned; a translation arranged with such consummate skill that, as the mind grows in spirituality, every stage of advance is met by a corresponding unfolding of the Divine meaning; while yet even the crudest apprehension of the idea implied is sufficient to afford the required basis for an entire renovation of the man's thoughts concerning himself, giving him a standing ground from which to think of himself as no longer bound by the law of retribution for past offences, but as free to follow out the new law of Liberty as a child of God.

The man's conception of the *modus operandi* of this emancipation may take the form of the grossest anthropomorphism or the most childish notions as to the satisfaction of the Divine justice by vicarious substitution, but the working result will be the same. He has got what satisfies him as a ground for thinking of himself in a perfectly new light; and since the states of our subjective consciousness constitute the realities of our life, to afford him a convincing ground for *thinking* himself free, is to make him free.

With increasing light he may find that his first explanation of the *modus operandi* was inadequate; but when he reaches this stage, further investigation will show him that the great truth of his liberty rests upon a firmer foundation than the conventional interpretation of traditional dogmas, and that it has its roots in the great law of Nature, which are never doubtful, and which can never be overturned. And it is precisely because their whole action has its root in the unchangeable laws of Mind that there exists a perpetual necessity for presenting to men something which they can lay hold of as a sufficient ground for that change of mental attitude, by which alone they can be rescued from the fatal circle which is figured under the symbol of the Old Serpent.

The hope and adumbration of such a new principle has formed the substance of all religions in all ages, however misapprehended by the ignorant worshippers; and, whatever our individual opinions may be as to the historical facts of Christianity, we shall find that the great figure of liberated and perfected humanity which forms its centre fulfils this desire of all nations in that it sets forth their great ideal of Divine power intervening to rescue man by becoming one with him. This is the conception presented to us, whether we apprehend it in the most literally material sense, or as the ideal presentation of the deepest philosophic study of mental laws, or in whatever variety of ways we may combine these two extremes. The ultimate idea impressed upon the mind must always be the same: it is that there is a Divine warrant for knowing ourselves to be the children of God and "partakers of the Divine nature"; and when we thus realize that there is solid ground for *believing* ourselves free, by force of this very belief we *become* free.

The proper outcome of the study of the laws of spirit which constitute the inner side of things is not the gratification of a mere idle curiosity, nor the acquisition of abnormal powers, but the attainment of our spiritual liberty, without which no further progress is possible. When we have reached this goal the old things have passed away and all things have become new. The mystical seven days of the old creation have been fulfilled, and the first day of the new week dawns upon us with its resurrection to a new life, expressing on the highest plane that great doctrine of the "octave" which the science of the ancient temples traced through Nature, and which the science of the present day endorses, though ignorant of its supreme significance.

When we have thus been made free by recognizing our oneness with Infinite Being, we have reached the termination of the old series of sequences and have gained the starting-point of the new. The old limitations are found never to have had any existence save in our own misapprehension of the truth, and one by one they fall off as we advance into clearer light. We find that the Life-Spirit we seek is *in ourselves*; and, having this for our centre, our relation to all else becomes part of a wondrous living Order in which every part works in sympathy with the whole, and the whole in sympathy with every part, a harmony wide as infinitude, and in which there are no limitations save those imposed by the Law of Love.

I have endeavored in this short series of articles to sketch briefly the principal points of relation between Spirit in ourselves and in our surroundings. This subject has employed the intelligence of mankind from grey antiquity to the present day, and no one thinker can ever hope to grasp it in all its amplitude. But there are certain broad principles which we must all grasp, however we may specialize our studies in detail, and these I have sought to indicate, with what degree of success the reader must form his own opinion. Let him, however, lay firm hold of this one fundamental truth, and the evolution of further truth from it is only a question of time—that there is only One Spirit, however many the modes of its manifestations, and that "the Unity of the Spirit is the Bond of Peace."

Chapter II

The Perversion of Truth

There is a very general recognition, which is growing day by day more and more widespread, that there is a sort of hidden power somewhere which it is within our ability, somehow or other, to use. The ideas on this subject are exceedingly vague with the generality of people, but still they are assuming a more and more definite form, and that which they appear to be taking with the generality of the public is the recognition of the power of suggestion. I suppose none of us doubts that there is such a thing as the power of suggestion and that it can produce very great results indeed, and that it is *par excellence* a hidden power; it works behind the scenes, it works through what we know as the subconscious mind, and consequently its activity is not immediately recognizable, or the source from which it comes. Now there is in some aspects, its usefulness, its benefit, but in other aspects there is a source of danger, because a power of this kind is obviously one which can be used either well or ill; in itself it is perfectly neutral, it all depends on the purpose for which it is used, and the character of the agent who employs it.

This recognition of the power of suggestion is in many instances taking a most undesirable form, and I commend to your notice, in support of this observation, numerous advertisements in certain classes of magazines—many of you must have seen many specimens of that kind—offering for a certain sum of money to put you in the way of getting personal influence, mental power, power of suggestion, as the advertisements very unblushingly put it, for any purpose that you may desire. Some of them even go into further particulars, telling you the particular sort of purposes for which you can employ this, all of them certainly being such uses as no one should ever attempt to make of it.

Therefore, this recognition of the power of suggestion, say even as a mere money-making power, to leave alone other misapplications of it, is a feature which is taking hold, so to say, of certain sections of the public who do not realize a higher platform in these things. It is deplorable that it should be so, but it is in the nature of things unavoidable. You have a power which can be used affirmatively, and which can be used negatively, which can be used for higher purposes, and can be used for lower purposes, and consequently you will find numbers of people who, as soon as they get hold of it, will at once think only of the lower purposes, not of the higher.

In support of what I say—although this is by no means, I suppose, intended as a low application, probably it is intended as a high application, but I cannot say I agree with it—but to show you that I am talking from actual facts I will read you a note which I have made from the *Daily Mail*, of the 20th January, that I daresay some of you may have seen. It is an article headed "Killing by Prayer," and the article goes on to say that a certain circular has been sent round to the different hospitals and other places where the study of vivisection goes forward to this effect. In this circular, signed with the letters "M. C.," the writer says that he accidentally heard of a person who was in the habit of praying from time to time for the death of one of our leading vivisectors and that always the man indicated died. That is what M. C. heard by chance during conversation at a hotel dinner. Then thinking over this, M. C. goes on to say that he (or she) tried praying that the man most likely to cause suffering to innocent subjects by his experiments might be removed, and the consequence was that about a fortnight later one of our most distinguished medical scientists died.

I do not know who the scientist in question was; I daresay some of you may be aware of the name. However, that is what the *Daily Mail* tells us, and it also states that the Anti-Vivisection Societies were unanimous in condemning this circular, and very properly so. Now you see the sender of that circular, whoever he was, obviously thought he was doing a very good piece of work. I myself am by no means any friend of vivisection. I do not think any one can have a real knowledge of the truth and remain in touch with it, but I certainly agreed with the Anti-Vivisection Societies in condemning such a circular as that. You see there is the assumption that prayer, or mental power, can be used to remove a person from the stage of life, and M. C. claims that he did it in the case of this particular scientist.

That brings back another parallel, almost, I might say, an historical parallel, to our mind; that of Dr. Anna Kingsford, taking place perhaps some forty years ago, who claimed—of course she was a very strong anti-vivisectionist—that by thought-power she caused the death of Claude Bernard, the great vivisection scientist of France. Certainly at the time that she put out her forces he did die, but on the other hand, it has been remarked that it was from that very date that her own break-up commenced, and never ceased till she herself passed into the other world. So you see these actions are likely to revert to the sender, even if they are successful.

Now in these two cases the ultimate object was not a low one, it was one which was supposed to be for the benefit of humanity and of the dumb creation. But that does not justify the means. The maxim, "The end justifies the means," is the greatest perversion of truth, and still more so if this hidden power, the power of suggestion, is used to injure any one for a more personal motive than in these cases which I have cited. The lower the motive, the lower the action becomes, and to suppose that because mental means are employed they make any difference in the nature of the act is a very great mistake.

It has been sometimes my painful duty to sentence people to death for murder, and therefore I claim that I have a very fair knowledge of what differentiates murder from those cases in which life is taken which do not amount to murder; and speaking from the judicial experience of a great many years, and the trial of a large number of cases which have involved the question whether the death penalty should be passed or not, I have no hesitation in saying that to kill by mental means is just as much murder as to kill by poison or the dagger. Speaking judicially, I should have not the least hesitation in hanging any one who committed murder by means of mental suggestion. Psychological crime, remember, is crime just the same; possibly it is more deeply dyed crime, because of the greater knowledge which must go along with it. I say that the psychological criminal is worse than the ordinary criminal.

One of the teachings of the Master is on this very point. I refer you to the miracle of the fig tree. You know that he exhibited his power of killing not a person, not even an animal, but a tree. And when the disciples said to him, see how this tree which you cursed has withered away, he replied, Well, you can do exactly the same thing, and goes on to say, nothing shall be impossible to you. Therefore if you can kill fig trees, you can kill people, but, "forgive, if you have aught against any," that your heavenly Father may forgive you.

He says in effect: now you have seen that this hidden power can be used to the destruction of life, at your peril use it otherwise than as a Divine power. Use it with prayer to God and with forgiveness of all against whom you have any sort of grudge or ill-feeling, and if its use is always prefaced in this way, according to the Master's directions, then nobody can use it to injure another either in mind, body or estate.

Perhaps some of you may be inclined to smile if I use the word "sorcery," but at the present day, under one name or another, scientific or semi-scientific, it is nothing but the old-world sorcery which is trying to find its way among us as the hidden power. Sorcery is the inverted use of spiritual power. That is the definition of it, and I speak upon authority. I refer you to the Bible where you will find sorcery takes a prominent place among the list of those things which exclude from the heavenly Jerusalem; the heavenly Jerusalem not being a town or a city in this place or that place, but the perfected state of man. Therefore, use sorcery, and you cannot reach that heavenly state.

It is on this account that we find in Revelations that wonderful description of two symbolical women; they represent two modes of the individual soul. Of course they go further, they indicate national things, race evolution and so on. Why? Because all national movements, all race evolutions, have their root in the development of the individual. A nation or a race is only a collection of individuals, and therefore if a principle once spreads from one individual to another, it spreads to the nation, it spreads to the race. So, therefore, these two symbolical women represent primarily two modes of soul, two modes of thought. You know perfectly well the description of the two women. One, the woman clothed with the sun, standing with the moon under her feet, and with a diadem of stars about her head; the other seated upon an earthly throne, holding a golden cup, and the cup is full of abominations. Those are the two women, and we know that one of them is called in the Scripture, Babylon, and we know which one that is. One of the marks of this woman—mind you that means the class of individuality—is the mark of sorcery, the mark of the inverted use of spiritual and mental powers.

But what is the end of it? The end is that this Babylon becomes the habitation of devils, the hold—or, as the original Greek has it, the prison of evil, an unclean spirit, the cage of every unclean bird. That is the development which takes place in each individual who sets out to misuse this mental power. The misuse may have a very small beginning, it may be such as is taught in a certain school, which I am told exists in London, where shop assistants are trained in the use of magnetic power, in order to decoy or compel unknowing purchasers into buying what they do not want. I am told there is such a school; I cannot quote you my authority. That is a trifling matter. I go into a shop and spend two or three shillings in buying something which, when I get home, I find absolutely useless, and I say, "How in the name of fortune did I come to buy this rubbish?" Well, I must have been hypnotized into it. It does not make much difference to me, but it makes a great deal of difference to the young man or young woman who has hypnotized me, because it is the first step on the downward path. It may be only a matter of sixpence, but it leads on step by step, and unless that path is retraced, the final end is that of Babylon. Therefore it is that St. John says, "I heard a voice from Heaven saying, 'Come forth, my people, out of her'"—and that is out of Babylon—"come forth, my people, out of her"—that is out of this inverted mode of using spiritual power—"come forth, my people, out of her, that ye have no fellowship with her sins and that ye shall receive not of her plague." Therefore, against this inverted use of the hidden power I warn every one from the first day when he begins to realize that there is such a thing as mental or spiritual power which can be exercised upon other persons.

Are we then on this account to go continually in terror of suffering from malicious magnetism, fearing that some enemy here, or some enemy there, is turning on this hidden power against us? If so, we should go in trepidation continually. No, I do not think there is the least reason for us to go in fear in this way. To begin with there are comparatively few who know the law of suggestion sufficiently well to use it either affirmatively or negatively, and of those who do know it sufficiently to make use of it, I am convinced that the majority would wish only to use it in all kindness, and for the benefit of the person concerned. That, I am confident, is the attitude of nine-tenths, or I might perhaps say ninety-nine hundredths, of the students of this subject. They wish to do well, and look upon their use of mental power as an additional means of doing good. But after all, human nature is human nature, and there remains a small minority who are both able and willing to use this hidden power injuriously for their own purposes.

Now how are we to deal with this minority? The answer is simple. Just see them in their true light, see them for what they really are, that is to say, persons who are ignorant of the real spiritual power. They think they have it, and they have not. That is what it is. See them in their true light and their power will fall away from them. The real and ultimate power is that of the affirmative; the negative is destructive, the affirmative is constructive. So this negative use of the hidden power is to be destroyed by the use of the affirmative, the constructive power. The affirmative destroys the negative always in one way, and that is not by attacking it, not by running at it like a bull in a china shop; but by building up life. It is always a building power—it is building, building, building life and more life, and when that life comes in, the negative of necessity goes out.

The ultimate affirmative position is that of conscious union with the source of life. Realize this, and you need not trouble yourself about any action of the negative whatever. Seek conscious union with the ultimate, the first cause, that which is the starting point of all things, whether in the universe or in yourself as the individual. That starting point is always present; it is the same yesterday, to-day and forever, and you are the world and the universe in miniature, and it is always there working in you if you will recognize it. Remember the reciprocity between yourself and this truly hidden power. The power of suggestion is *a* hidden power, but the power which creates all things is *the* hidden power which is at the back of all things. Now realize that it is in yourselves and you need trouble about the negative no longer. This is the Bible teaching regarding Christ; and that teaching is to bring about this conscious personal union with the Divine All-creating Spirit as a present living power to be used day by day.

The Bible tells us there is such a thing as the mystery of iniquity, that is to say, the mystery of the spiritual power used invertedly, used from the diabolical standpoint; and when the Bible speaks of the mystery of iniquity, it means what it says. It tells us there are powers and principalities in the invisible world which are using precisely these same methods on an enormous scale; because, remember one thing, there is never any departure in any part of the Universe from the universal rule of law; what is law upon earth is law in Heaven, law in Hell, law in the invisible and law in the visible; that never alters. What is done by any spiritual power, whether it is a spiritual power of evil or of good, is done through the mental constitution which you have. No power alters the law of your own mind, but a power which knows the law of your mind can use it.

Therefore, it is so essential that you should know the law of your own mind and realize its continual amenability to suggestion. That being so, the great thing is to get a standard for fundamental, unchangeable, and sufficient suggestion to which you can always turn, and which is automatically impressed upon your subconscious mind so deeply that no counter-suggestion can ever take its place; and that is the mystery of Christ, the Son of God. That is why we are told of the mystery of Christ, the mystery of godliness in opposition to the mystery of iniquity; it is because both the mystery of the Divine and the mystery of the diabolical are seeking to work through you, and they can only work through you by the law of your own mental constitution, that is to say, by the law of subconscious mind acting and re-acting upon your conscious mind and upon your body, and so upon your circumstances.

The mystery of Christ is no mere ecclesiastical fiction. People have distorted it, and made it not clear, by trying to explain what at that time and in those days was not properly known, by trying to explain what they did not know; because what is commonly now known regarding the laws of mind was unknown then. But now this light has come we begin to see that the Bible teaching regarding Christ has a great and a deep meaning, and it is for these reasons St. Paul said to the Corinthians: "Little children of whom I travail again in birth, until Christ be formed in you." That is why he speaks of "Christ in you the hope of glory," that is to say, the Christ conception, the realization of the Christ principle as exhibited in the Christ person, brings you in touch with the personal element in the Universal Spirit, the divine creative, first moving Spirit of the Universe.

Then you see that realizing this as your fundamental fact, it is continually impressed upon your subconscious mind, even when you are not thinking of it, because that is the action of the subconscious mind to take in and reason and argue in its own deductive way upon things of which you are not at the moment consciously thinking. Therefore it is that the realization of that great promise of redemption, which is the backbone of the Bible from the first chapter of Genesis to the last chapter of Revelations, is according to a scientific law. It is not a hocus-pocus business, it is not a thing which has been arranged this way and might just as well have been arranged in some other; it is not so because some arbitrary Authority has commanded it, and the Authority might just as well have commanded it some other way.

No, it is so because the more you examine it, the more you will find that it is absolutely scientific; it is based upon the natural constitution of the human mind. And it is therefore that "Christ," as set forth in the Bible—whether in the Old Testament symbology, or in the New Testament personality—"is the fulfilling of the law," in the sense of specializing in the highest degree that which is common to all humanity. As we realize this more and more, and specialize it more and more, so we shall rise to higher and higher intercourse and more and more consciousness of reciprocal identity, reciprocal life with the Universal Power, which will raise us above any possibility of being touched by any sort of malicious suggestion.

If anybody should be, then, so ill-willed towards us and so lamentably ignorant of spiritual truth himself as to seek to exercise the power of malicious suggestion against us, I pity the person who tries to do it. He will get nothing out of it, because he is firing peas out of a pea-shooter against an iron-clad war vessel. That is what it amounts to; but for himself it amounts to something more. It is a true saying that "Curses return home to roost." I think if we study these things, and consider that there is a reason for them, we need not be in the least alarmed about negative suggestion, or malicious magnetism, of being brought under the power of other minds, of being got over in some way, of being done out of our property, of being injured in our health, or being hurt in our circumstances, and so on.

Of course if you lay yourself open to that kind of thing, you will get it. "Knock, and it shall be opened unto you." That is why the Scripture says, "He that breaketh through a hedge, a serpent shall bite him." That is the serpent that some of us know something about, that is our old enemy Nahash. Some of you, at any rate, are sufficiently trained in the inner sciences to know the serpent Nahash. Break down the hedge, that is to say, the conscious control of your own mind, and above all the hedge of the Divine love and wisdom with which God himself will surround you in the personality of His Son, break down this hedge and of course Nahash comes in. But if you keep your hedge—and remember the old Hebrew tradition always spoke of the Divine Law as "the hedge"—if you keep your hedge unbroken, nothing can come in except by the door. Christ said, "I am the door, by me if any man enter in, he shall be saved."

I have spoken of the two great mysteries, the mystery of godliness and the mystery of iniquity, the mystery of Christ and the mystery of anti-Christ. Now, it is not necessary, mind you, that you should understand these mysteries in full in order to get into your right position. If it were necessary that we should fully understand these mysteries, either to get away from the one or to get into the other, I think all of us would have an uncommonly bad chance. I certainly should. I can touch only the fringe of these things, but we can realize the principle of the affirmative and the principle of the negative which underlies them both; one is the mystery of light, the other is the mystery of darkness.

I do not say do not study these mysteries; they are exactly what we ought to study, but do not think that you remain in a state of danger until you have completely fathomed the mystery. Not a bit of it. You can quite get on the right side without understanding the whole thing, exactly as you travel on a railway without understanding the mechanism of the engine which takes you along.

So then we have these two mysteries, that of light and that of darkness, and therefore what we have to do is to exercise our will to receive the mystery of light, and then that will make for itself a centre in our own hearts and beings, and you will become conscious of that centre. Whether you understand it or not, you will become conscious of it—and then from that centre, that centre of light in yourself, you can start everything in your life, whether spiritual or temporal. You do not have to go further back; you do not have to analyze the why and the wherefore of these things in order to get your starting point. It may interest you afterwards, it may strengthen you afterwards to do so, but for a practical starting point you must realize the Divine presence in yourself, which is the son of God manifested in you, that is the Divine principle of personality speaking within yourself.

So then, having realized this as your centre, you carry the all-originating affirmative power with you, all through everything that you do and everything that you are; day and night it will be there, it will protect you, it will guide you, it will help you. And when you want to do so you can consciously apply to it and it will give you assistance, and because you take this as your starting point, it will manifest itself in all your conditions; because, remember, it is a very simple law of logic that whatever you start with will manifest itself all down the sequence which comes from it. If you start with the color red you can make all sorts of modifications and bring out orange, purple and brown, but the red basis will show itself all down the scale of color, and so if you start with a basis of blue, blue will show itself all down the scale of various colors.

Therefore, if you start with the affirmative basis, the one starting point of the Divine spirit, not taking it lower down the stream, but going to the fountain head, that affirmative principle of life will flow all through, showing its own quality to the very tips of your fingers and beyond that out into all your circumstances. So that the divine presence will be continuously with you, not as a consequence of your joining this Church or that, following this idea, or that teacher, but because you know the truth for yourselves, and you have realized it as an actual living experience in your own mind and in your own heart; and therefore it is that this personal recognition of the Divine love and wisdom and power is what St. Paul calls "Christ in you, the hope of glory."

Each one who recognizes this, is one who answers the Biblical description of a true Israelite indeed. That word "Israelite" in the Bible is a very deeply symbolical word, and carries an immense amount of meaning with it. So get this recognition as the real working fact that each one of you is an Israelite indeed, and if so, then make yourselves perfectly happy with the everlasting statement, which is as true now as it was on the day on which it was uttered: "There is no divination or enchantment against Israel."

1909.

Chapter III

The "I Am"

We often do not sufficiently recognize the truth of Walt Whitman's pithy saying, "I am not all contained between my hat and my boots," and forget the two-fold nature of the "I AM," that it is at once both the manifested and the unmanifested, the universal and the individual. By losing sight of this truth we surround ourselves with limitations; we see only part of the self, and then we are surprised that the part fails to do the work of the whole. Factors crop up on which we had not reckoned, and we wonder where they come from, and do not understand that they necessarily arise from that great unity in which we are all included.

It is the grand intelligence and livingness of Universal Spirit continually pressing forward to manifestation of itself in a glorious humanity.

This must be effected by each individual's recognition of his power to co-operate with the Supreme Principle through an intelligent conception of its purpose and of the natural laws by which that purpose is accomplished—a recognition which can proceed only from the realization that he himself is none other than the same Universal Principle in particular manifestation.

When he sees this he sees that Walt Whitman's saying is true, and that his source of intelligence, power, and purpose is in that Universal Self, which is his as well as another's just because it is universal, and which is therefore as completely and entirely identified with himself as though there were no other expression of it in the world.

The understanding which alone gives value to knowledge is the understanding that, when we employ the formula "I am, therefore I can, therefore I will," the "I AM" with which the series starts is a being who, so to speak, has his head in heaven and his feet upon the earth, a perfect unity, and with a range of ideas far transcending the little ideas which are limited by the requirements of a day or an hour. On the other hand, the requirements of the day and the hour are real while they last, and since the manifested life can be lived only in the moment that now is, whether it be to-day or ten thousand years hence, our need is to harmonies the life of expression with the life of purpose, and by realizing in ourselves the source of the highest purposes to realize also the life of the fullest expression.

This is the meaning of prayer. Prayer is not a foolish seeking to change the mind of Supreme Wisdom, but it is an intelligent seeking to embody that wisdom in our thoughts so as more and more perfectly to express *it* in expressing *ourselves*. Thus, as we gradually grow into the habit of finding this inspiring Presence *within ourselves*, and of realizing its forward movement as the ultimate determining factor in all true healthful mental action, it will become second nature to us to have all our plans, down to the apparently most trivial, so floating upon the undercurrent of this Universal Intelligence that a great harmony will come into our lives, every discordant manifestation will disappear, and we shall find ourselves more and more controlling all things into the forms that we desire.

Why? Because we have attained to *commanding* the Spirit and making it obey us? Certainly not, for "if the blind lead the blind both shall fall into the ditch"; but because we are *companions* of the Spirit, and by a continuous and growing intimacy have changed, not "the mind of the Spirit," but our own, and have learned to think from a higher standpoint, where we see that the old-world saying "know thyself" includes the knowledge of all that we mean when we speak of God.

I AM IS ONE

This may seem a very elementary proposition, but it is one of which we are too apt to lose sight. What does it mean? It means everything; but we are most concerned with what it means in regard to ourselves, and to each of us personally it means this. It means that there are not two Spirits, one which is myself and one which is another. It means that there is not some great unknown power external to myself which may be actuated by perfectly different motives to my own, and which will, therefore, oppose me with its irresistible force and pass over me, leaving me crushed and broken like the devotee over whom the car of Jaggarnath has rolled. It means that there is only one mind, one motive, one power—not two opposing each other—and that my conscious mind in all its movements is only the one mind expressing itself as (not merely through) my own particular individuality.

There are not two I AMS, but one I am. Whatever, therefore, I can conceive the Great Universal Life Principle to be, that I am. Let us try fully to realize what this means. Can you conceive the Great Originating and Sustaining Life Principle of the whole universe as poor, weak, sordid, miserable, jealous, angry, anxious, uncertain, or in any other way limited? We know that this is impossible. Then because the I AM is one it is equally untrue of ourselves. Learn first to distinguish the true self that you are from the mental and physical processes which it throws forth as the instruments of its expression, and then learn that this self controls these instruments, and not vice versa. As we advance in this knowledge we know ourselves to be unlimited, and that, in the miniature world, whose centre we are, we ourselves are the very same overflowing of joyous livingness that the Great Life Spirit is in the Great All. The I AM is One.

Chapter IV

Affirmative Power

Thoroughly to realize the true nature of affirmative power is to possess the key to the great secret. We feel its presence in all the innumerable forms of life by which we are surrounded and we feel it as the life in ourselves; and at last some day the truth bursts upon us like a revelation that we can wield this power, this life, by the process of Thought. And as soon as we see this, the importance of regulating our thinking begins to dawn upon us. We ask ourselves what this thought process is, and we then find that it is thinking affirmative force into forms which are the product of our own thought. We mentally conceive the form and then think life into it.

This must always be the nature of the creative process on whatever scale, whether on the grand scale of the Universal Cosmic Mind or on the miniature scale of the individual mind; the difference is only in degree and not in kind. We may picture the mental machinery by which this is done in the way that best satisfies our intellect—and the satisfying of the intellect on this point is a potent factor in giving us that confidence in our mental action without which we can effect nothing—but the actual externalization is the result of something more powerful than a merely intellectual apprehension. It is the result of that inner mental state which, for want of a better word, we may call our emotional conception of ourselves. It is the "self" which we *feel* ourselves to be which takes forms of our own creating. For this reason our thought must be so grounded upon knowledge that we shall *feel* the truth of it, and thus be able to produce in ourselves that mental attitude of feeling which corresponds to the condition which we desire to externalize.

We cannot think into manifestation a different sort of life to that which we realize in ourselves. As Horace says, "*Nemo dat quod non habet*," we cannot give what we have not got. And, on the other hand, we can never cease creating forms of some sort by our mental activity, thinking life into them. This point must be very carefully noted. We cannot sit still producing nothing: the mental machinery *will* keep on turning out work of some sort, and it rests with us to determine of what sort it shall be. In our entire ignorance or imperfect realization of this we create negative forms and think life into them. We create forms of death, sickness, sorrow, trouble, and limitation of all sorts, and then think life into these forms; with the result that, however non-existent in themselves, to us they become realities and throw their shadow across the path which would otherwise be bright with the many-colored beauties of innumerable flowers and the glory of the sunshine.

This need not be. It is giving to the negative an affirmative force which does not belong to it. Consider what is meant by the negative. It is the absence of something. It is not-being, and is the absence of all that constitutes being. Left to itself, it remains in its own nothingness, and it only assumes form and activity when we give these to it by our thought.

Here, then, is the great reason for practicing control over our thought. It is the one and only instrument we have to work with, but it is an instrument which works with the greatest certainty, for limitation if we think limitation, for enlargement if we think enlargement. Our thought as feeling is the magnet which draws to us those conditions which accurately correspond to itself. This is the meaning of the saying that "thoughts are things." But, you say, how can I think differently from the circumstances? Certainly you are not required to say that the circumstances *at the present moment* are what they are not; to say so would be untrue; but what is wanted is not to think from the standpoint of circumstances at all. Think from that interior standpoint where there are no circumstances, and from whence you can dictate what circumstances shall be, and then leave the circumstances to take care of themselves.

Do not think of this, that, or the other particular *circumstances* of health, peace, etc., but of health, peace, and prosperity themselves. Here is an advertisement from *Pearson's Weekly*:—"Think money. Big moneymakers *think* money." This is a perfectly sound statement of the power of thought, although it is only an advertisement; but we may make an advance beyond thinking "money." We can think "Life" in all its fullness, together with that perfect harmony of conditions which includes all that we need of money and a thousand other good things besides, for some of which money stands as the symbol of exchangeable value, while others cannot be estimated by so material a standard.

Therefore think Life, illumination, harmony, prosperity, happiness—think the things rather than this or that condition of them. And then by the sure operation of the Universal Law these things will form themselves into the shapes best suited to your particular case, and will enter your life as active, living forces, which will never depart from you because you know them to be part and parcel of your own being.

Chapter V

Submission

There are two kinds of submission: submission to superior force and submission to superior truth. The one is weakness and the other is strength. It is an exceedingly important part of our training to learn to distinguish between these two, and the more so because the wrong kind is extolled by nearly all schools of popular religious teaching at the present day as constituting the highest degree of human attainment. By some this is pressed so far as to make it an instrument of actual oppression, and with all it is a source of weakness and a bar to progress. We are forbidden to question what are called the wise dispensations of Providence and are told that pain and sorrow are to be accepted because they are the will of God; and there is much eloquent speaking and writing concerning the beauty of quiet resignation, all of which appeals to a certain class of gentle minds who have not yet learnt that gentleness does not consist in the absence of power but in the kindly and beneficent use of it.

Minds cast in this mould are peculiarly apt to be misled. They perceive a certain beauty in the picture of weakness leaning upon strength, but they attribute its soothing influence to the wrong element of the combination. A thoughtful analysis would show them that their feelings consisted of pity for the weak figure and admiration for the strong one, and that the suggestiveness of the whole arose from its satisfying the artistic sense of balance which requires a compensation of this sort. But which of the two figures in the picture would they themselves prefer to be? Surely not the weak one needing help, but the strong one giving it. By itself the weak figure only stirs our pity and not our admiration. Its form may be beautiful, but its very beauty only serves to enhance the sense of something wanting—and the something wanting is strength. The attraction which the doctrine of passive resignation possesses for certain minds is based upon an appeal to sentiment, which is accepted without any suspicion that the sentiment appealed to is a false one.

Now the healthful influence of the movement known as "The Higher Thought" consists precisely in this—that it sets itself rigorously to combat this debilitating doctrine of submission. It can see as well as others the beauty of weakness leaning upon strength; but it sees that the real source of the beauty lies in the strong element of the combination. The true beauty consists in the power to confer strength, and this power is not to be acquired by submission, but by the exactly opposite method of continually asserting our determination not to submit.

Of course, if we take it for granted that all the sorrow, sickness, pain, trouble, and other adversity in the world is the expression of the will of God, then doubtless we must resign ourselves to the inevitable with all the submission we can command, and comfort ourselves with the vague hope that somehow in some far-off future we shall find that

"Good is the final goal of ill,"

though even *this* vague hope is a protest against the very submission we are endeavoring to exercise. But to make the assumption that the evil of life is the will of God is to assume what a careful and intelligent study of the laws of the universe, both mental and physical, will show us is not the truth; and if we turn to that Book which contains the fullest delineation of these universal laws, we shall find nothing taught more clearly than that submission to the evils of life is not submission to the will of God. We are told that Christ was manifested for this end, that he should destroy him that hath the power of death—that is, the devil. Now death is the very culmination of the Negative. It is the entire absence of all that makes Life, and whatever goes to diminish the living quality of Life reproduces, in its degree, the distinctive quality of this supreme exhibition of the Negative. Everything that tends to detract from the fullness of life has in it this deathful quality.

In that completely renovated life, which is figured under the emblem of the New Jerusalem, we are told that sorrow and sighing shall flee away, and that the inhabitant shall not say, I am sick. Nothing that obscures life, or restricts it, can proceed from the same source as the Power which gives light to them that sit in darkness, and deliverance to them that are bound. Negation can never be Affirmation; and the error we have always to guard against is that of attributing positive power to the Negative. If we once grasp the truth that God is life, and that life in every mode of expression can never be anything else than Affirmative, then it must become clear to us that nothing which is of the opposite tendency can be according to the will of God. For God (the good) to will any of the "evil" that is in the world would be for Life to act with the purpose of diminishing itself, which is a contradiction in terms to the very idea of Life. God is Life, and Life is, by its very nature, Affirmative. The submission we have hitherto made has been to our own weakness, ignorance, and fear, and not to the supreme good.

But is no such thing as submission, then, required of us under any circumstances? Are we always to have our own way in everything? Assuredly the whole secret of our progress to liberty is involved in acquiring the habit of submission; but it is submission to superior Truth, and not to superior force. It sometimes happens that, when we attain a higher Truth, we find that its reception requires us to re-arrange the truths which we possessed before: not, indeed, to lay any of them aside, for Truth once recognized cannot be again put out of sight, but to recognize a different relative proportion between them from that which we had seen previously. Then there comes a submitting of what has hitherto been our highest truth to one which we recognize as still higher, a process not always easy of attainment, but which must be gone through if our spiritual development is not to be arrested. The lesser degree of life must be swallowed up in the greater; and for this purpose it is necessary for us to learn that the smaller degree was only a partial and limited aspect of that which is more universal, stronger, and of a larger build every way.

Now, in going through the processes of spiritual growth, there is ample scope for that training in self-knowledge and self-control which is commonly understood by the word "submission." But the character of the act is materially altered. It is no longer a half-despairing resignation to a superior force external to ourselves, which we can only vaguely hope is acting kindly and wisely, but it is an intelligent recognition of the true nature of our own interior forces and of the laws by which a robust spiritual constitution is to be developed; and the submission is no longer to limitations which drain life of its livingness, and against which we instinctively rebel, but to the law of our own evolution which manifests itself in continually increasing degrees of life and strength.

The submission which we recognize is the price that has to be paid for increase in any direction. Even in the Money Market we must invest before we can realize profits. It is a universal rule that Nature obeys us exactly in proportion as we first obey Nature; and this is as true in regard to spiritual science as to physical. The only question is whether we will yield an ignorant submission to the principle of Death, or a joyous and intelligent obedience to the principle of Life.

If we have clearly grasped the fact of our identity with Universal Spirit, we shall find that, in the right direction, there is really no such thing as submission. Submission is to the power of another—a man cannot be said to submit to himself. When the "I AM" in us recognizes a greater degree of I AM-ness (if I may coin the word) than it has hitherto attained, then, by the very force of this recognition, it *becomes what it sees*, and therefore naturally puts off from itself whatever would limit its expression of its own completeness.

But this is a natural process of growth, and not an unnatural act of submission; it is not the pouring-out of ourselves in weakness, but the gathering of ourselves together in increasing strength. There is no weakness in Spirit, it is all strength; and we must therefore always be watchful against the insidious approaches of the Negative which would invert the true position. The Negative always points to some external source of strength. Its formula is "I AM NOT." It always seeks to fix a gulf between us and the Infinite

Sufficiency. It would always have us believe that that sufficiency is not our own, but that by an act of uncertain favor we may have occasional spoonfuls of it doled out to us. Christ's teaching is different. We do not need to come with our pitcher to the well to draw water, like the woman of Samaria, but we have *in ourselves* an inexhaustible supply of the living water springing up into everlasting life.

Let us then inscribe "No Surrender" in bold characters upon our banner, and advance undaunted to claim our rightful heritage of liberty and life.

Chapter VI

Completeness

A point on which students of mental science often fail to lay sufficient stress is the completeness of man—not a completeness to be attained hereafter, but here and now. We have been so accustomed to have the imperfection of man drummed into us in books, sermons, and hymns, and above all in a mistaken interpretation of the Bible, that at first the idea of his completeness altogether staggers us. Yet until we see this we must remain shut out from the highest and best that mental science has to offer, from a thorough understanding of its philosophy, and from its greatest practical achievements.

To do any work successfully you must believe yourself to be a *whole* man in respect of it. The completed work is the outward image of a corresponding completeness in yourself. And if this is true in respect of one work it is true of all; the difference in the importance of the work does not matter; we cannot successfully attempt *any* work until, for some reason or other, we believe ourselves able to accomplish it; in other words, until we believe that none of the conditions for its completion is wanting in us, and that we are therefore complete in respect of it. Our recognition of our completeness is thus the measure of what we are able to do, and hence the great importance of knowing the fact of our own completeness.

But, it may be asked, do we not see imperfection all around? Is there not sorrow, sickness, and trouble? Yes; but why? Just for the very reason that we do not realize our completeness. If we realized *that* in its fullness these things would not be; and in the degree in which we come to realize it we shall find them steadily diminish. Now if we really grasp the two fundamental truths that Spirit is Life pure and simple, and that external things are the result of interior forces, then it ought not to be difficult to see why we should be complete; for to suppose otherwise is to suppose the reactive power of the universe to be either unable or unwilling to produce the complete expression of its own intention in the creation of man.

That it should be unable to do so would be to depose it from its place as the creative principle, and that it should be unwilling to fulfill its own intention is a contradiction in terms; so that on either supposition we come to a *reductio ad absurdum*. In forming man the creative principle therefore *must* have produced a perfect work, and our conception of ourselves as imperfect can only be the result of our own ignorance of what we really are; and our advance, therefore, does not consist in having something new added to us, but in learning to bring into action powers which already exist in us, but which we have never tried to use, and therefore have not developed, simply because we have always taken it for granted that we are by nature defective in some of the most important faculties necessary to fit us to our environment.

If we wish to attain to these great powers, the question is, where are we to seek them? And the answer is *in ourselves*. That is the great secret. We are not to go outside ourselves to look for power. As soon as we do so we find, not power, but weakness. To seek strength from any outside source is to make affirmation of our weakness, and all know what the natural result of such an affirmation must be.

We are complete *in ourselves*; and the reason why we fail to realize this is that we do not understand how far the "self" of ourselves extends. We know that the whole of anything consists of *all* its parts and not only of some of them; yet this is just what we do not seem to know about ourselves. We say rightly that every person is a concentration of the Universal Spirit into individual consciousness; but if so, then each individual consciousness must find the Universal Spirit to be the infinite expression of *itself*. It is *this* part of the "Self" that we so often leave out in our estimate of what we are; and consequently we look upon ourselves as crawling pygmies when we might think of ourselves as archangels. We try to work with the mere shadows of ourselves instead of with the glorious substance, and then wonder at our failures. If we only understood that our "better half" is the whole infinite of Spirit—that which creates and sustains the universe—then we should know how complete our completeness is.

As we approach this conception, our completeness becomes a reality to us, and we find that we need not go outside ourselves for anything. We have only to draw on that part of ourselves which is infinite to carry out any intention we may form in our individual consciousness; for there is no barrier between the two parts, otherwise they would not be a whole. Each belongs perfectly to the other, and the two are one. There is no antagonism between them, for the Infinite Life can have no interest against its individualization of *itself*. If there is any feeling of tension it proceeds from our not fully realizing this conception of our own wholeness; we are placing a barrier somewhere, when in truth there is none; and the tension will continue until we find out where and how we are setting up this barrier and remove it.

This feeling of tension is the feeling that we are *not using our Whole Being*. We are trying to make half do the work of the whole; but we cannot rid ourselves of our wholeness, and therefore the whole protests against our attempts to set one half against the other. But when we realize that our concentration *out of* the Infinite also implies our expansion *into* it, we shall see that our *whole* "self" includes both the concentration and the expansion;

and seeing this first intellectually we shall gradually learn to use our knowledge practically and bring our whole man to bear upon whatever we take in hand. We shall find that there is in us a constant action and reaction between the infinite and the individual, like the circulation of the blood from the heart to the extremities and back again, a constant pulsation of vital energy quite natural and free from all strain and exertion.

This is the great secret of the livingness of Life, and it is called by many names and set forth under many symbols in various religions and philosophies, each of which has its value in proportion as it brings us nearer the realization of this perfect wholeness. But the thing itself is Life, and therefore can only be suggested, but not described, by any words or symbols; it is a matter of personal experience which no one can convey to another. All we can do is to point out the direction in which this experience is to be sought, and to tell others the intellectual arguments which have helped us to find it; but the experience itself is the operation of definite vital functions of the inner being, and no one but ourselves can do our living for us.

But, so far as it is possible to express these things in words, what must be the result of realizing that the "self" in us includes the Infinite as well as the Individual? All the resources of the Infinite must be at our disposal; we may draw on them as we will, and there is no limit save that imposed by the Law of Kindness, a self-imposed limitation, which, because of being *self*-imposed, is not bondage but only another expression of our liberty. Thus we are free and all limitations are removed.

We are also no longer ignorant, for since the "self" in us includes the Infinite we can draw thence all needed knowledge, and though we may not always be able to formulate this knowledge in the mentality, we shall *feel* its guidance, and eventually the mentality will learn to put this also into form of words; and thus by combining thought and experience, theory and practice, we shall by degrees come more and more into the knowledge of the Law of our Being, and find that there is no place in it for fear, because it is the law of perfect liberty. And knowing what our whole self really is, we shall walk erect as free men and women radiating Light and Life all round, so that our very presence will carry a vivifying influence with it, because we realize ourselves to be an Affirmative Whole, and not a mere negative disintegration of parts.

We know that our whole self includes that Greater Man which is back of and causes the phenomenal man, and this Greater Man is the true human principle in us. It is, therefore, universal in its sympathies, but at the same time not less individually *ourself*; and thus the true man in us, being at once both universal and individual, can be trusted as a sure guide. It is that "Thinker" which is behind the conscious mentality, and which, if we will accept it as our centre, and realize that it is not a separate entity but *ourself*, will be found equal to every occasion, and will lead us out of a condition of servitude into "the glorious liberty of the sons of God."

Chapter VII

The Principle of Guidance

If I were asked which of all the spiritual principles ranked first, I should feel inclined to say the Principle of Guidance; not in the sense of being more essential than the others, for *every* portion is equally essential to the completeness of a perfect whole, but in the sense of being first in order of sequence and giving value to all our other powers by placing them in their due relation to one another. "Giving value to our *other* powers," I say, because this also is one of our powers. It is that which, judged from the standpoint of personal self-consciousness, is above us; but which, realized from the point of view of the unity of all Spirit, is part and parcel of ourselves, because it is that Infinite Mind which is of necessity identified with all its manifestations.

Looking to this Infinite Mind as a Superior Intelligence from which we may receive guidance does not therefore imply looking to an external source. On the contrary, it is looking to the innermost spring of our own being, with a confidence in its action which enables us to proceed to the execution of our plans with a firmness and assurance that are in themselves the very guarantee of our success.

The action of the spiritual principles in us follows the order which we impose upon them by our thought; therefore the order of realization will reproduce the order of desire; and if we neglect this first principle of right order and guidance, we shall find ourselves beginning to put forth other great powers, which are at present latent within us, without knowing how to find suitable employment for them—which would be a very perilous condition, for without having before us objects worthy of the powers to which we awake, we should waste them on petty purposes dictated only by the narrow range of our unilluminated intellect. Therefore the ancient wisdom says, "With all thy getting, get understanding."

The awakening to consciousness of our mysterious interior powers will sooner or later take place, and will result in our using them whether we understand the law of their development or not, just as we already use our physical faculties whether we understand their laws or not. The interior powers are natural powers as much as the exterior ones. We can direct their use by a knowledge of their laws; and it is therefore of the highest importance to have some sound principle of guidance in the use of these higher faculties as they begin to manifest themselves.

If, therefore, we would safely and profitably enter upon the possession of the great inheritance of power that is opening out before us, we must before all things seek to realize in ourselves that Superior Intelligence which will become an unfailing principle of guidance if we will only recognize it as such. Everything depends on our recognition. Thoughts are things, and therefore as we *will* our thoughts to be so we *will* the thing to be. If, then, we will to use the Infinite Spirit as a spirit of guidance, we shall find that the fact is as we have willed it; and in doing this we are still making use of our own supreme principle. And this is the true "understanding" which, by placing all the other powers in their correct order, creates one grand unity of power directed to clearly defined and worthy aims, in place of the dispersion of our powers, by which they only neutralize each other and effect nothing.

This is that Spirit of Truth which shall guide us into all Truth. It is the sincere Desire of us reaching out after Truth. Truth first and Power afterwards is the reasonable order, which we cannot invert without injury to ourselves and others; but if we follow this order we shall always find scope for our powers in developing into present realities the continually growing glory of our vision of the ideal.

The ideal is the true real, but it must be brought into manifestation before it can be shown to be so, and it is in this that the *practical* nature of our mental studies consists. It is the *practical* mystic who is the man of power; the man who, realizing the mystical powers within, fits his outward action to this knowledge, and so shows his faith by his works; and assuredly the first step is to make use of that power of infallible guidance which he can call to his aid simply by desiring to be led by it.

Chapter VIII

Desire as the Motive Power

There are certain Oriental schools of thought, together with various Western offshoots from them, which are entirely founded on the principle of annihilating all desire. Reach that point at which you have no wish for anything and you will find yourself free, is the sum and substance of their teaching; and in support of this they put forward a great deal of very specious argument, which is all the more likely to entangle the unwary, because it contains a recognition of many of the profoundest truths of Nature. But we must bear in mind that it is possible to have a very deep knowledge of psychological facts, and at the same time vitiate the results of our knowledge by an entirely wrong assumption in regard to the law which binds these facts together in the universal system; and the injurious results of misapprehension upon such a vital question are so radical and far-reaching that we cannot too forcibly urge the necessity of clearly understanding the true nature of the point at issue. Stripped of all accessories and embellishments, the question resolves itself into this: Which shall we choose for our portion, Life or Death? There can be no accommodation between the two; and whichever we select as our guiding principle must produce results of a kind proper to itself.

The whole of this momentous question turns on the place that we assign to desire in our system of thought. Is it the Tree of Life in the midst of the Garden of the Soul? or is it the Upas Tree creating a wilderness of death all around? This is the issue on which we have to form a judgment, and this judgment must color all our conception of life and determine the entire range of our possibilities. Let us, then, try to picture to ourselves the ideal proposed by the systems to which I have alluded—a man who has succeeded in entirely annihilating all desire. To him all things must be alike. The good and the evil must be as one, for nothing has any longer the power to raise any desire in him; he has no longer any feeling which shall prompt him to say, "This is good, therefore I choose it; that is evil, therefore I reject it"; for all choice implies the perception of something more desirable in what is chosen than in what is rejected, and consequently the existence of that feeling of desire which has been entirely eliminated from the ideal we are contemplating.

Then, if the perception of all that makes one thing preferable to another has been obliterated, there can be no motive for any sort of action whatever. Endue a being who has thus extinguished his faculty of desire with the power to create a universe, and he has no motive for employing it. Endue him with all knowledge, and it will be useless to him; for, since desire has no place in him, he is without any purpose for which to turn his knowledge to account. And with Love we cannot endue him, for that is desire in its supreme degree. But if all this be excluded, what is left of the man? Nothing, except the mere outward form. If he has actually obtained this ideal, he has practically ceased to be. Nothing can by any means interest him, for there is nothing to attract or repel in one thing more than in another. He must be dead alike to all feeling and to all motive of action, for both feeling and action imply the preference for one condition rather than another; and where desire is utterly extinguished, no such preference can exist.

No doubt some one may object that it is only evil desires which are thus to be suppressed; but a perusal of the writings of the schools of thought in question will show that this is not the case. The foundation of the whole system is that *all* desire must be obliterated, the desire for the good just as much as the desire for the evil. The good is as much "illusion" as the evil, and until we have reached absolute indifference to both we have not attained freedom. When we have utterly crushed out *all* desire we are free. And the practical results of such a philosophy are shown in the case of Indian devotees, who, in pursuance of their resolve to crush out *all* desire, both for good and evil alike, become nothing more than outward images of men, from which all power of perception and of action have long since fled.

The mergence in the universal, at which they thus aim, becomes nothing more than a self-induced hypnotism, which, if maintained for a sufficient length of time, saps away every power of mental and bodily activity, leaving nothing but the outside husk of an attenuated human form—the hopeless wreck of what was once a living man. This is the logical result of a system which assumes for its starting-point that desire is evil in itself, that every desire is *per se* a form of bondage, independently of the nature of its object. The majority of the followers of this philosophy may lack sufficient resolution to carry it out rigorously to its practical conclusions; but whether their ideal is to be realized in this world or in some other, the utter extinction of desire means nothing else than absolute apathy, without feeling and without action.

How entirely false such an idea is—not only from the standpoint of our daily life, but also from that of the most transcendental conception of the Universal Principle—is evidenced by the mere fact that anything exists at all. If the highest ideal is that of utter apathy, then the Creative Power of the universe must be extremely low-minded; and all that we have hitherto been accustomed to look upon as the marvelous order and beauty of creation, is nothing but a display of vulgarity and ignorance of sound philosophy.

But the fact that creation exists proves that the Universal Mind thinks differently, and we have only to look around to see that the true ideal is the exercise of creative power. Hence, so far from desire being a thing to be annihilated, it is the very root of every conceivable mode of Life. Without it Life could not be. Every form of expression implies the selection of all that goes to make up that form, and the passing-by of whatever is not required for that purpose; hence a desire for that which is selected in preference to what is laid aside. And this selective desire is none other than the universal Law of Attraction.

Whether this law acts as the chemical affinity of apparently unconscious atoms, or in the instinctive, if unreasoned, attractions of the vegetable and animal worlds, it is still the principle of selective affinity; and it continues to be the same when it passes on into the higher kingdoms which are ruled by reason and conscious purpose. The modes of activity in each of these kingdoms are dictated by the nature of the kingdom; but the activity itself always results from the preference of a certain subject for a certain object, to the exclusion of all others; and all action consists in the reciprocal movement of the two towards each other in obedience to the law of their affinity.

When this takes place in the kingdom of conscious individuality, the affinities exhibit themselves as mental action; but the principle of selection prevails without exception throughout the universe. In the conscious mind this attraction towards its affinity becomes desire; the desire to create some condition of things better than that now existing. Our want of knowledge may cause us to make mistakes as to what this better thing really is, and so in seeking to carry out our desire we may give it a wrong direction; but the fault is not in the desire itself, but in our mistaken notion of what it is that it requires for its satisfaction. Hence unrest and dissatisfaction until its true affinity is found; but, as soon as this is discovered, the law of attraction at once asserts itself and produces that better condition, the dream of which first gave direction to our thoughts.

Thus it is eternally true that desire is the cause of all feeling and all action; in other words, of all Life. The whole livingness of Life consists in receiving or in radiating forth the vibrations produced by the law of attraction; and in the kingdom of mind these vibrations necessarily become conscious out-reachings of the mind in the direction in which it feels attraction; that is to say, they become desires. Desire is therefore the mind seeking to manifest itself in some form which as yet exists only in its thought. It is the principle of creation, whether the thing created be a world or a wooden spoon; both have their origin in the desire to bring something into existence which does not yet exist. Whatever may be the scale on which we exercise our creative ability, the motive power must always be desire.

Desire is the force behind all things; it is the moving principle of the universe and the innermost centre of all Life. Hence, to take the negation of desire for our primal principle is to Endeavour to stamp out Life itself; but what we have to do is to acquire the requisite knowledge by which to guide our desires to their true objects of satisfaction. To do this is the whole end of knowledge; and any knowledge applied otherwise is only a partial knowledge, which, having failed in its purpose, is nothing but ignorance. Desire is thus the sum-total of the livingness of Life, for it is that in which all movement originates, whether on the physical level or the spiritual. In a word, desire is the creative power, and must be carefully guarded, trained, and directed accordingly; but thus to seek to develop it to the highest perfection is the very opposite of trying to kill it outright.

And desire has fulfillment for its correlative. The desire and its fulfillment are bound together as cause and effect; and when we realize the law of their sequence, we shall be more than ever impressed with the supreme importance of Desire as the great centre of Life.

Chapter IX
Touching Lightly

What is our point of support? Is it in ourselves or outside us? Are we self-poised, or does our balance depend on something external? According to the actual belief in which our answer to these questions is embodied so will our lives be. In everything there are two parts, the essential and the incidental—that which is the nucleus and *raison d'être* of the whole thing, and that which gathers round this nucleus and takes form from it. The true knowledge always consists in distinguishing these two from each other, and error always consists in misplacing them.

In all our affairs there are two factors, ourselves and the matter to be dealt with; and since *for us* the nature of anything is always determined by our thought of it, it is entirely a question of our belief which of these two factors shall be the essential and which the accessory. Whichever we regard as the essential, the other at once becomes the incidental. The incidental can never be absent. For any sort of action to take place there must be *some* conditions under which the activity passes out into visible results; but the same sort of activity may occur under a variety of different conditions, and may thus produce very different visible results. So in every matter we shall always find an essential or energizing factor, and an incidental factor which derives its quality from the nature of the energy.

We can therefore never escape from having to select our essential and our incidental factor, and whichever we select as the essential, we thereby place the other in the position of the incidental. If, then, we make the mistake of reversing the true position and suppose that the energizing force comes from the merely accessory circumstances, we make *them* our point of support and lean upon *them*, and stand or fall with them accordingly; and so we come into a condition of weakness and obsequious waiting on all sorts of external influences, which is the very reverse of that strength, wisdom, and opulence which are the only meaning of Liberty.

But if we would ask ourselves the common-sense question Where can the centre of a man's Life be except in himself? we shall see that in all which pertains to us the energizing centre must be in ourselves. We can never get away from ourselves as the centre of our own universe, and the sooner we clearly understand this the better. There is really no energy in *our* universe but what emanates from ourselves in the first instance, and the power which appears to reside in our surroundings is derived entirely from our own mind.

If once we realize this, and consider that the Life which flows into us from the Universal Life-Principle is at every moment *new* Life entirely undifferentiated to any particular purpose besides that of supporting our own individuality, and that it is therefore ours to externalize in any form we will, then we find that this manifestation of the eternal Life-Principle *in ourselves* is the standpoint from which we can control our surroundings. We must lean firmly on the central point of our own being and not on anything else. Our mistake is in taking our surroundings too much "*au grand serieux.*" We should touch things more lightly. As soon as we feel that their weight impedes our free handling of them they are mastering us, and not we them.

Light handling does not mean weak handling. On the contrary, lightness of touch is incompatible with a weak grasp of the instrument, which implies that the weight of the tool is excessive relatively to the force that seeks to guide it. A light, even playful handling, therefore implies a firm grasp and perfect control over the instrument. It is only in the hands of a Grinling Gibbons that the carving tool can create miracles of aerial lightness from the solid wood. The light yet firm touch tells not of weakness, but of power held in reserve; and if we realize our own out-and-out spiritual nature we know that behind any measure of power we may put forth there is the whole reserve of the infinite to back us up.

As we come to know this we begin to handle things lightly, playing with them as a juggler does with his flying knives, which cannot make the slightest movement other than he has assigned to them, for we begin to see that our control over things is part of the necessary order of the universe. The disorder we have met with in the past has resulted precisely from our never having attempted consciously to introduce this element of our personal control as part of the system.

Of course, I speak of the *whole* man, and not merely of that part of him which Walt Whitman says is contained between his hat and his boots. The *whole* man is an infinitude, and the visible portion of him is the instrument through which he looks out upon and enjoys all that belongs to him, his own kingdom of the infinite. And when he learns that this is the meaning of his conscious individuality, he sees *how* it is that he is infinite, and finds that he is one with Infinite Mind, which is the innermost core of the universe. Having thus reached the true centre of his own being, he can never give this central place to anything else, but will realize that relatively to this all other things are in the position of the incidental and accessory, and growing, daily in this knowledge he will learn so to handle all things lightly, yet firmly, that grief, fear, and error will have less and less space in his world, until at last sorrow and sighing shall flee away, and everlasting joy shall take their place. We may have taken only a few steps on the way as yet, but they are in the right direction, and what we have to do now is to go on.

Chapter X

Present Truth

If Thought power is good for anything it is good for everything. If it can produce one thing it can produce all things. For what is to hinder it? Nothing can stop us from thinking. We can *think* what we please, and if to think is to form, then we can form what we please. The whole question, therefore, resolves itself into this: Is it true that to think is to form? If so, do we not see that our limitations are formed in precisely the same way as our expansions? We think that conditions outside our thought have power over us, and so we think power into them. So the great question of life is whether there is any *other* creative power than Thought. If so, where is it, and what is it?

Both philosophy and religion lead us to the truth that "in the beginning" there was no other creative power than Spirit, and the only mode of activity we can possibly attribute to Spirit is Thought, and so we find Thought as the root of all things. And if this was the case "in the beginning" it must be so still; for if all things originate in Thought, all things must be modes of Thought, and so it is impossible for Spirit ever to hand over its creations to some power which is not itself—that is to say, which is not Thought-power; and consequently all the forms and circumstances that surround us are manifestations of the creative power of Thought.

But it may be objected that this is God's Thought; and that the creative power is in God and not Man. But this goes away from the self-evident axiomatic truth that "in the beginning" nothing could have had any origin except Thought. It is quite true that nothing has any origin except in the Divine Mind, and Man himself is therefore a mode of the Divine Thought. Again, Man is self-conscious; therefore Man is the Divine Thought evolved into *individual* consciousness, and when he becomes sufficiently enlightened to realize this as his origin, then he sees that he is a reproduction *in individuality* of the *same* spirit which produces all things, and that his own thought in individuality has exactly the same quality as the Divine Thought in universality, just as fire is equally igneous whether burning round a large centre of combustion or a small one, and thus we are logically brought to the conclusion that our thought must have creative power.

But people say, "We have not found it so. We are surrounded by all sorts of circumstances that we do not desire." Yes, you *fear* them, and in so doing you *think* them; and in this way you are constantly exercising this Divine prerogative of creation by Thought, only through ignorance you use it in a wrong direction. Therefore the Book of Divine Instructions so constantly repeats "Fear not; doubt not," because we can never divest our Thought of its inherent creative quality, and the only question is whether we shall use it ignorantly to our injury or understandingly to our benefit.

The Master summed up his teaching in the aphorism that knowledge of the Truth would make us free. Here is no announcement of anything we have to do, or of anything that has to be done for us, in order to gain our liberty, neither is it a statement of anything *future*. Truth *is* what is. He did not say, you must wait till something becomes true which is not true *now*. He said: "Know what *is* Truth now, and you will find that the Truth concerning yourself is Liberty." If the knowledge of Truth makes us free it can only be because in truth we are free already, only we do not know it.

Our liberty consists in our reproducing on the scale of the individual the same creative power of Thought which first brought the world into existence, "so that the things which are seen were not made of things which do appear." Let us, then, confidently claim our birthright as "sons and daughters of the Almighty," and by habitually thinking the good, the beautiful, and the true, surround ourselves with conditions corresponding to our thoughts, and by our teaching and example help others to do the same.

Chapter XI

Yourself

I want to talk to you about the livingness there is in being yourself. It has at least the merit of simplicity, for it must surely be easier to be oneself than to be something or somebody else. Yet that is what so many are constantly trying to do; the self that is their own is not good enough for them, and so they are always trying to go one better than what God has made them, with endless strain and struggle as the consequence. Of course, they are right to put before them an ideal infinitely grander than anything they have yet attained—the only possible way of progress is by following an ideal that is always a stage ahead of us—but the mistake is in not seeing that its attainment is a matter of growth, and that growth must be the expansion of something that already exists in us, and therefore implies our being what we are and where we are as its starting point. This growth is a continuous process, and we cannot do next month's growth without first doing this month's; but we are always wanting to jump into some ideal of the future, not seeing that we can reach it only by steadily going on from where we are now.

These considerations should make us more confident and more comfortable. We are employing a force which is much greater than we believe ourselves to be, yet it is not separate from us and needing to be persuaded or compelled, or inveigled into doing what we want; it is the substratum of our own being which is continually passing up into manifestation on the visible plane and becoming that personal self to which we often limit our attention without considering whence it proceeds. But in truth the outer self is the surface growth of that individuality which lies concealed far down in the deeps below, and which is none other than the Spirit-of-Life which underlies all forms of manifestation.

Endeavour to realize what this Spirit must be in itself—that is to say, apart from any of the conditions that arise from the various relations which necessarily establish themselves between its various forms of individualization. In its homogeneous self what else can it be but pure life—Essence-of-Life, if you like so to call it? Then realize that as Essence-of-Life it exists in the innermost of *every one* of its forms of manifestation in as perfect simplicity as any we can attribute to it in our most abstract conceptions. In this light we see it to be the eternally self-generating power which, to express itself, flows into form.

This universal Essence-of-Life is a continual becoming (into form), and since we are a part of Nature we do not need to go further than ourselves to find the life-giving energy at work with all its powers. Hence all we have to do is to allow it to rise to the surface. We do not have to *make* it rise any more than the engineer who sinks the bore-pipe for an artesian well has to make the water rise in it; the water does that by its own energy, springing as a fountain a hundred feet into the air. Just so we shall find a fountain of Essence-of-Life ready to spring up in ourselves, inexhaustible and continually increasing in its flow, as One taught long ago to a woman at a wayside well.

This up-springing of Life-Essence is not another's—it is our own. It does not require deep studies, hard labors, weary journeying to attain it; it is not the monopoly of this teacher or that writer, whose lectures we must attend or whose books we must read to get it. It is the innermost of *ourselves*, and a little common-sense thought as to how anything comes to be anything will soon convince us that the great inexhaustible life must be the very root and substance of us, permeating every fiber of our being.

Surely to be this vast infinitude of living power must be enough to satisfy all our desires, and yet this wonderful ideal is nothing else but what we already are *in principio*—it is all there in ourselves now, only awaiting our recognition for its manifestation. It is not the Essence-of-Life which has to grow, for that is eternally perfect in itself; but it is our recognition of it that has to grow, and this growth cannot be forced. It must come by a natural process, the first necessity of which is to abstain from all straining after being something which at the present time we cannot naturally be. The Law of our Evolution has put us in possession of certain powers and opportunities, and our further development depends on our doing just what these powers and opportunities make it possible for us to do, here and now.

If we do what we are able to do to-day, it will open the way for us to do something better to-morrow, and in this manner the growing process will proceed healthily and happily in a rapidly increasing ratio. This is so much easier than striving to compel things to be what they are not, and it is also so much more fruitful in good results. It is not sitting still doing nothing, and there is plenty of room for the exercise of all our mental faculties, but these faculties are themselves the outcome of the Essence-of-Life, and are not the creating power, but only that which gives direction to it Now it is this moving power at the back of the various faculties that is the true innermost self; and if we realize the identity between the innermost and the outermost, we shall see that we therefore have at our present disposal all that is necessary for our unlimited development in the future.

Thus our livingness consists simply in being ourselves, only more so; and in recognizing this we get rid of a great burden of unnecessary straining and striving, and the place of the old *sturm und drang* will be taken, not by inertia, but by a joyous activity which knows that it always has the requisite power to manifest itself in forms of good and beauty. What matters it whither this leads us? If we are following the line of the beautiful and good, then we shall produce the beautiful and good, and thus bring increasing joy into the world, whatever particular form it may assume.

We limit ourselves when we try to fix accurately beforehand the particular form of good that we shall produce. We should aim not so much at having or making some particular thing as at expressing all that we are. The expressing will grow out of realizing the treasures that are ours already, and contemplating the beauty, the affirmative side, of all that we are *now*, apart from the negative conceptions and detractions which veil this positive good from us. When we do this we shall be astonished to see what possibilities reside in ourselves as we are and with our present surroundings, all unlovely as we may deem them: and commencing to work at once upon whatever we find of affirmative in these, and withdrawing our thought from what we have hitherto seen of negative in them, the right road will open up before us, leading us in wonderful ways to the development of powers that we never suspected, and the enjoyment of happiness that we never anticipated.

We have never been out of our right path, only we have been walking in it backwards instead of forwards, and now that we have begun to follow the path in the right direction, we find that it is none other than the way of peace, the path of joy, and the road to eternal life. These things we may attain by simply living naturally with ourselves. It is because we are trying to be or do something which is not natural to us that we experience weariness and labor, where we should find all our activities joyously concentrated on objects which lead to their own accomplishment by the force of the love that we have for them. But when we make the grand discovery of how to live naturally, we shall find it to be all, and more than all, that we had ever desired, and our daily life will become a perpetual joy to ourselves, and we shall radiate light and life wherever we go.

Chapter XII

Religious Opinions

That great and wise writer, George Eliot, expressed her matured views on the subject of religious opinions in these words: "I have too profound a conviction of the efficacy that lies in all sincere faith, and the spiritual blight that comes with no faith, to have any negative propagandism left in me." This had not always been her attitude, for in her youth she had had a good deal of negative propagandism in her; but the experience of a lifetime led her to form this estimate of the value of sincere faith, independently of the particular form of thought which leads to it.

Tennyson also came to the same conclusion, and gives kindly warning:—

"O thou who after toil and storm
May'st seem to have reached a purer air,
Whose faith has centred everywhere,
Nor cares to fix itself to form.
Leave thou thy sister when she prays
Her early heaven, her happy views,
Nor thou with shadowed hint confuse
A life that leads melodious days."

And thus these two great minds have left us a lesson of wisdom which we shall do well to profit by. Let us see how it applies more particularly to our own case.

The true presentment of the Higher Thought contains no "negative propagandism." It is everywhere ranged on the side of the Affirmative, and its great object is to extirpate the canker which gnaws at the root of every life that endeavors to centre itself upon the Negative. Its purpose is constructive and not destructive. But we often find people laboring under a very erroneous impression as to the nature and scope of the movement, and thus not only themselves deterred from investigating it, but also deterring others from doing so. Sometimes this results from the subject having been presented to them unwisely—in a way needlessly repugnant to the particular form of religious ideas to which they are accustomed; but more often it results from their prejudging the whole matter, and making up their minds that the movement is opposed to their ideas of religion, without being at the pains to inquire what its principles really are. In either case a few words on the attitude of the New Thought towards the current forms of religious opinion may not be out of place.

The first consideration in every concern is, What is the object aimed at? The end determines the means to be employed, and if the nature of the end be clearly kept in view, then no objectless complications will be introduced into the means. All this seems too obvious to be stated, but it is just the failure to realize this simple truth that has given rise to the whole body of *odium theologicum*, with all the persecutions and massacres and martyrdoms which disgrace the pages of history, making so many of them a record of nothing but ferocity and stupidity. Let us hope for a better record in the future; and if we are to get it, it will be by the adoption of the simple principle here stated.

In our own country alone the varieties of churches and sects form a lengthy catalogue, but in every one of them the purpose is the same—to establish the individual in a satisfactory relation to the Divine Power. The very fact of any religious profession at all implies the recognition of God as the Source of life and of all that goes to make life; and therefore the purpose in every case is to draw increasing degrees of life, whether here or hereafter, from the Only Source from which alone it is to be obtained, and therefore to establish such a relation with this Source as may enable the worshipper to draw from It all the life he wants. Hence the necessary preliminary to drawing consciously at all is the confidence that such a relation actually has been established; and such a confidence as this is exactly all that is meant by Faith.

The position of the man who has not this confidence is either that no such Source exists, or else that he is without means of access to It; and in either case he feels himself left to fight for his own hand against the entire universe without the consciousness of any Superior Power to back him up. He is thrown entirely upon his own resources, not knowing of the interior spring from which they may be unceasingly replenished. He is like a plant cut off at the stem and stuck in the ground without any root, and consequently that spiritual blight of which George Eliot speaks creeps over him, producing weakness, perplexity, and fear, with all their baleful consequences, where there should be that strength, order, and confidence which are the very foundation of all building-up for whatever purpose, whether of personal prosperity or of usefulness to others.

From the point of view of those who are acquainted with the laws of spiritual life, such a man is cut off from the root of his own Being. Beyond and far interior to that outer self which each of us knows as the intellectual man working with the physical brain as instrument, we have roots penetrating deep into that Infinite of which, in our ordinary waking state, we are only dimly conscious; and it is through this root of our own individuality, spreading far down into the hidden depths of Being, that we draw out of the unseen that unceasing stream of Life which afterwards, by our thought-power, we differentiate into all those outward forms of which we have need. Hence the unceasing necessity for every one to realize the great truth that his whole individuality has its foundation in such a root, and that the ground in which this root is embedded is that Universal Being for which there is no name save that of the One all-embracing I AM.

The supreme necessity, therefore, for each of us is to realize this fundamental fact of our own nature, for it is only in proportion as we do so that we truly live; and, therefore, whatever helps us to this realization should be carefully guarded. In so far as any form of religion contributes to this end in the case of any particular individual, for him it is true religion. It may be imperfect, but it is true so far as it goes; and what is wanted is not to destroy the foundation of a man's faith because it is narrow, but to expand it. And this expanding will be done by the man himself, for it is a growth from within and not a construction from without.

Our attitude towards the religious beliefs of others should, therefore, not be that of iconoclasts, breaking down ruthlessly whatever from *our* point of view we see to be merely traditionary idols (in Bacon's sense of the word), but rather the opposite method of fixing upon that in another's creed which we find to be positive and affirmative, and gradually leading him to perceive in what its affirmativeness consists; and then, when once he has got the clue to the element of strength which exists in his accustomed form of belief, the perception of the contrast between that and the non-essential accretions will grow up in his mind spontaneously, thus gradually bringing him out into a wider and freer atmosphere. In going through such a process as this, he will never have had his thoughts directed into any channel to suggest separation from his spiritual root and ground; but he will learn that the rooting and grounding in the Divine, which he had trusted in at first, were indeed true, but in a sense far fuller, grander, and larger every way than his early infantile conception of them.

The question is not how far can another's religious opinions stand the test of a remorseless logic, but how far do they enable him to realize his unity with Divine Spirit? That is the living proof of the value of his opinion to himself, and no change in his opinions can be for the better that does not lead him to a greater recognition of the livingness of Divine Spirit in himself. For any change of opinion to indicate a forward movement, it must proceed from our realizing in some measure the true nature of the life that is already developed in us. When we see *why* we are *what* we are *now*, then we can look ahead and see what the same life principle that has brought us up to the present point is capable of doing in the future. We may not see very far ahead, but we shall see where the next step is to be placed, and that is sufficient to enable us to move on.

What we have to do, therefore, is to help others to grow from the root they are already *living* by, and not to dig their roots up and leave them to wither. We need not be afraid of making ourselves all things to all men, in the sense of fixing upon the affirmative elements in each one's creed as the starting-point of our work, for the affirmative and life-giving is always true, and Truth is always *one* and consistent with itself; and therefore we need never fear being inconsistent so long as we adhere to this method. It is worse than useless to waste time in dissecting the negative accretions of other people's beliefs. In doing so we run great risks of rooting up the wheat along with the tares, and we shall certainly succeed in brushing people up the wrong way; moreover, by looking out exclusively for the life-giving and affirmative elements, we shall reap benefit to ourselves. We shall not only keep our temper, but we shall often find large reserves of affirmative power where at first we had apprehended nothing but worthless accumulations, and thus we shall become gainers both in largeness of mind and in stores of valuable material.

Of course we must be rigidly unyielding as regards the *essence* of Truth—*that* must never be sacrificed—but as representatives, in however small a sphere, of the New Thought, we should make it our aim to show others, not that their religion is wrong, but that all they may find of life-givingness in it is life-giving because it is part of the One Truth which is always the same under whatever form expressed. As half a loaf is better than no bread, so ignorant worship is better than no worship, and ignorant faith is better than no faith. Our work is not to destroy this faith and this worship, but to lead them on into a clearer light.

For this reason we may assure all inquirers that the abandonment of their customary form of worship is no necessity of the New Thought; but, on the contrary, that the principles of the movement, correctly understood, will show them far more meaning in that worship than they have ever yet realized. Truth is one; and when once the truth which underlies the outward form is clearly understood, the maintenance or abandonment of the latter will be found to be a matter of personal feeling as to what form, or absence of form, best enables the particular individual to realize the Truth itself.

Chapter XIII

A Lesson from Browning

Perhaps you know a little poem of Browning's called "An Epistle Containing the Strange Medical Experiences of Karshish, the Arab Physician." The somewhat weird conception is that the Arab physician, travelling in Palestine soon after the date when the Gospel narrative closes, meets with Lazarus whom Jesus raised from the dead, and in this letter to a medical friend describes the strange effect which his vision of the other life has produced upon the resuscitated man. The poem should be studied as a whole; but for the present a few lines selected here and there must do duty to indicate the character of the change which has passed upon Lazarus. After comparing him to a beggar who, having suddenly received boundless wealth, is unable to regulate its use to his requirements, Karshish continues:—

"So here—we call the treasure knowledge, say,
Increased beyond the fleshly faculty—
Heaven opened to a soul while yet on earth,
Earth forced on a soul's use while seeing heaven:
The man is witless of the size, the sum,
The value in proportion of all things."

In fact he has become almost exclusively conscious of

"The spiritual life around the earthly life:
The law of that is known to him as this,
His heart and brain move there, his feet stay here,"

and the result is a loss of mental balance entirely unfitting him for the affairs of ordinary life.

Now there can be no doubt that Browning had a far more serious intention in writing this poem than just to record a fantastic notion that flitted through his brain. If we read between the lines, it must be clear from the general tenor of his writings that, however he may have acquired it, Browning had a very deep acquaintance with the inner region of spiritual causes which give rise to all that we see of outward phenomenal manifestation. There are continual allusions in his works to the life behind the veil, and it is to this suggestion of some mystery underlying his words that we owe the many attempts to fathom his meaning expressed through Browning Societies and the like—attempts which fail or succeed according as they are made from "the without" or from "the within." No one was better qualified than the poet to realize the immense benefits of the inner knowledge, and for the same reason he is also qualified to warn us of the dangers on the way to its acquisition; for nowhere is it more true that

"A little knowledge is a dangerous thing,"

and it is one of the greatest of these dangers that he points out in this poem.

Under the figure of Lazarus he describes the man who has practically grasped the reality of the inner side of things, for whom the veil has been removed, and who knows that the external and visible takes its rise from the internal and spiritual. But the description is that of one whose eyes have been so dazzled by the light that he has lost the power of accommodating his vision to the world of sense. He now commits the same error from the side of "the within" that he formerly committed from the side of "the without," the error of supposing that there is no vital reality in the aspect of things on which his thoughts are not immediately centered. This is want of mental balance, whether it shows itself by refusing reality to the inward or the outward. To be so absorbed in speculative ideas as to be unable to give them practical application in daily life, is to allow our highest thoughts to evaporate in dreams.

There is a world of philosophy in the simple statement that there can be no inside without an outside, and no outside without an inside; and the great secret in life is in learning to see things in their wholeness, and to realize the inside and the outside simultaneously. Each of them without the other is a mere abstraction, having no real existence, which we contemplate separately only for the purpose of reviewing the logical steps by which they are connected together as cause and effect. Nature does not separate them, for they are inseparable; and the law of nature is the law of life. It is related of Pythagoras that, after he had led his scholars to the dizziest heights of the inner knowledge, he never failed to impress upon them the converse lesson of tracing out the steps by which these inner principles translate themselves into the familiar conditions of the outward things by which we are surrounded. The process of analysis is merely an expedient for discovering what springs in the realm of causes we are to touch in order to produce certain effects in the realm of manifestation. But this is not sufficient. We must also learn to calculate how those particular effects, when produced, will stand related to the world of already existing effects among which we propose to launch them, how they will modify these and be modified by these in turn; and this calculation of effects is as necessary as the knowledge of causes.

We cannot impress upon ourselves too strongly that reality consists of both an inside and an outside, a generating principle and a generated condition, and that anything short of the reality of wholeness is illusion on one side or the other. Nothing could have been further from Browning's intention than to deter seekers after truth from studying the principles of Being, for without the knowledge of them truth must always remain wrapped in mystery; but the lesson he would impress on us is that of guarding vigilantly the mental equilibrium which alone will enable us to develop those boundless powers whose infinite unfolding is the fullness of Life. And we must remember above all that the soul of life is Love, and that Love shows itself by service, and service proceeds from sympathy, which is the capacity for seeing things from the point of view of those whom we would help, while at the same time seeing them also in their true relations; and therefore, if we would realize that Love which is the inmost vitalizing principle even of the most interior powers, it must be kept alive by maintaining our hold upon the exterior life as being equally real with the inward principles of which it is the manifestation.

1902.

Chapter XIV
The Spirit of Opulence

It is quite a mistake to suppose that we must restrict and stint ourselves in order to develop greater power or usefulness. This is to form the conception of the Divine Power as so limited that the best use we can make of it is by a policy of self-starvation, whether material or mental. Of course, if we believe that some form of self-starvation is necessary to our producing good work, then so long as we entertain this belief the fact actually is so *for us*. "Whatsoever is not of faith"—that is, not in accordance with our honest *belief*—"is sin"; and by acting contrary to what we really believe we bring in a suggestion of opposition to the Divine Spirit, which must necessarily paralyze our efforts, and surround us with a murky atmosphere of distrust and want of joy.

But all this exists in, and is produced by, our *belief*; and when we come to examine the grounds of this belief we shall find that it rests upon an entire misapprehension of the nature of our own power. If we clearly realize that the creative power in ourselves is *unlimited*, then there is no reason for limiting the extent to which we may enjoy what we can create by means of it. Where we are drawing from the *infinite* we need never be afraid of taking more than our share. That is not where the danger lies. The danger is in not sufficiently realizing our own richness, and in looking upon the externalized products of our creative power as being the true riches instead of the creative power of spirit itself.

If we avoid this error, there is no need to limit ourselves in taking what we will from the infinite storehouse: "All things are yours." And the way to avoid this error is by realizing that the true wealth is in identifying ourselves with the *spirit* of opulence. We must be opulent in our *thought*. Do not "think money," as such, for it is only one means of opulence; but *think opulence*, that is, largely, generously, liberally, and you will find that the means of realizing this thought will flow to you from all quarters, whether as money or as a hundred other things not to be reckoned in cash.

We must not make ourselves dependent on any particular *form* of wealth, or insist on its coming to us through some particular channel—that is at once to impose a limitation, and to shut out other forms of wealth and to close other channels; but we must enter into the *spirit* of it. Now the spirit is Life, and throughout the universe Life ultimately consists in *circulation*, whether within the physical body of the individual or on the scale of the entire solar system; and circulation means a continual flowing around, and the *spirit* of opulence is no exception to this universal law of all life.

When once this principle becomes clear to us we shall see that our attention should be directed rather to the giving than the receiving. We must look upon ourselves, not as misers' chests to be kept locked for our own benefit, but as centers of distribution; and the better we fulfill our function as such centers the greater will be the corresponding inflow. If we choke the outlet the current must slacken, and a full and free flow can be obtained only by keeping it open. The spirit of opulence—the opulent mode of thought, that is—consists in cultivating the feeling that we possess all sorts of riches which we can *bestow upon others*, and which we can bestow *liberally* because by this very action we open the way for still greater supplies to flow in. But you say, "I am short of money, I hardly know how to pay for necessaries. What have I to give?"

The answer is that we must always start from the point where we are; and if your wealth at the present moment is not abundant on the material plane, you need not trouble to start on that plane. There are other sorts of wealth, still more valuable, on the spiritual and intellectual planes, which you can give; and you can start from this point and practice the spirit of opulence, even though your balance at the bank may be nil. And then the universal law of attraction will begin to assert itself. You will not only begin to experience an inflow on the spiritual and intellectual planes, but it will extend itself to the material plane also.

If you have realized the *spirit* of opulence you *cannot help* drawing to yourself material good, as well as that higher wealth which is not to be measured by a money standard; and because you truly understand the *spirit* of opulence you will neither affect to despise this form of good, nor will you attribute to it a value that does not belong to it; but you will *co-ordinate* it with your other more interior forms of wealth so as to make it the material instrument in smoothing the way for their more perfect expression. Used thus, with understanding of the relation which it bears to spiritual and intellectual wealth, material wealth becomes *one with them*, and is no more to be shunned and feared than it is to be sought for its own sake.

It is not money, but the *love* of money, that is the root of evil; and the *spirit* of opulence is precisely the attitude of mind which is furthest removed from the love of money for its own sake. It does not believe in money. What it does believe in is the generous feeling which is the intuitive recognition of the great law of circulation, which does not in any undertaking make its first question, how much am I going to *get* by it? but, How much am I going to *do* by it? And making *this* the first question, the getting will flow in with a generous profusion, and with a spontaneousness and rightness of direction that are absent when our first thought is of receiving only.

We are not called upon to give what we have not yet got and to run into debt; but we are to give liberally of what we *have*, with the knowledge that by so doing we are setting the law of circulation to work, and as this law brings us greater and greater inflows of every kind of good, so our out-giving will increase, not by depriving ourselves of any expansion of our own life that we may desire, but by finding that every expansion makes us the more powerful instruments for expanding the life of others. "Live and let live" is the motto of the true opulence.

Chapter XV

Beauty

Do we sufficiently direct our thoughts to the subject of Beauty? I think not. We are too apt to regard Beauty as a merely superficial thing, and do not realize all that it implies. This was not the case with the great thinkers of the ancient world—see the place which no less a one than Plato gives to Beauty as the expression of all that is highest and greatest in the system of the universe. These great men of old were no superficial thinkers, and, therefore, would never have elevated to the supreme place that which is only superficial. Therefore, we shall do well to ask what it is that these great minds found in the idea of Beauty which made it thus appeal to them as the most perfect outward expression of all that lies deepest in the fundamental laws of Being. It is because, rightly apprehended, Beauty represents the supremest living quality of Thought. It is the glorious overflowing of fullness of Love which indicates the presence of infinite reserves of Power behind it. It is the joyous profusion that shows the possession of inexhaustible stores of wealth which can afford to be thus lavish and yet remain as exhaustless as before. Read aright, Beauty is the index to the whole nature of Being.

Beauty is the externalization of Harmony, and Harmony is the co-ordinated working of all the powers of Being, both in the individual and in the relation of the individual to the Infinite from which it springs; and therefore this Harmony conducts us at once into the presence of the innermost undifferentiated Life. Thus Beauty is in most immediate touch with the very arcanum of Life; it is the brightness of glory spreading itself over the sanctuary of the Divine Spirit. For if, viewed from without, Beauty is the province of the artist and the poet, and lays hold of our emotions and appeals directly to the innermost feelings of our heart, calling up the response of that within us which recognizes itself in the harmony perceived without, this is only because it speeds across the bridge of Reason with such quick feet that we pass from the outmost to the inmost and back again in the twinkling of an eye; but the bridge is still there and, retracing our steps more leisurely, we shall find that, viewed from within, Beauty is no less the province of the calm reasoner and analyst. What the poet and the artist seize upon intuitionally, he elaborates gradually, but the result is the same in both cases; for no intuition is true which does not admit of being expanded into a rational sequence of intelligible factors, and no argument is true which does not admit of being condensed into that rapid suggestion which is intuition.

Thus the impassioned artist and the calm thinker both find that the only true Beauty proceeds naturally from the actual construction of that which it expresses. It is not something added on as an afterthought, but something pre-existing in the original idea, something to which that idea naturally leads up, and which presupposes that idea as affording it any *raison d'être*. The test of Beauty is, What does it express? Is it merely a veneer, a coat of paint laid on from without? Then it is indeed nothing but a whited sepulcher, a covering to hide the vacuity or deformity which needs to be removed. But is it the true and natural outcome of what is beneath the surface? Then it is the index to super abounding Life and Love and Intelligence, which is not content with mere utilitarianism hasting to escape at the earliest possible point from the labor of construction, as though from an enforced and unwelcome task, but rejoicing over its work and unwilling to quit it until it has expressed this rejoicing in every fittest touch of form and color and exquisite proportion that the material will admit of, and this without departing by a hairbreadth from the original purpose of the design.

Wherever, therefore, we find Beauty, we may infer an enormous reserve of Power behind it; in fact, we may look upon it as the visible expression of the great truth that Life-Power is infinite. And when the inner meaning of Beauty is thus revealed to us, and we learn to know it as the very fullness and overflowing of Power, we shall find that we have gained a new standard for the guidance of our own lives. We must begin to use this wonderful process which we have learnt from Nature. Having learnt how Nature works—how God works—we must begin to work in like manner, and never consider any work complete until we have carried it to some final outcome of Beauty, whether material, intellectual, or spiritual. Is my intention good? That is the initial question, for the intention determines the nature of the essence in everything. What is the most beautiful form in which I can express the good I intend? That is the ultimate question; for the true Beauty which our work expresses is the measure of the Power, Intelligence, Love—in a word, of the quantity and quality of our own life which we have put into it. True Beauty, mind you—that which is beautiful because it most perfectly expresses the original idea, not a mere ornamentation occupying our thoughts as a thing apart from the use intended.

Nothing is of so small account but it has its fullest power of expression in some form of Beauty peculiarly its own. Beauty is the law of perfect Thought, be the subject of our Thought some scheme affecting the welfare of millions, or a word spoken to a little child. True Beauty and true Power are the correlatives one of the other. Kindly expression originates in kindly thought; and kindly expression is the essence of Beauty, which, seeking to express itself ever more and more perfectly, becomes that fine touch of sympathy which is artistic skill, whether applied in working upon material substances or upon the emotions of the heart. But, remember, first Use, then Beauty, and neither complete without the other. Use without Beauty is ungracious giving, and Beauty without Use is humbug; never forgetting, however, that there is a region of the mind where the use is found in the beauty, where Beauty itself serves the direct purpose of raising us to see a higher ideal which will thenceforward permeate our lives, giving a more living quality to all we think and say and do.

Seen thus the Beautiful is the true expression of the Good. From whichever end of the scale we look we shall find that they accurately measure each other. They are the same thing in the outermost and the innermost respectively. But in our search for a higher Beauty than we have yet found we must beware of missing the Beauty that already exists. Perfect harmony with its environment, and perfect expression of its own inward nature are what constitute Beauty; and our ignorance of the nature of the thing or its environment may shut our eyes to the Beauty it already has. It takes the genius of a Millet to paint, or a Whitman in words, to show us the beauty of those ordinary work-a-day figures with which our world is for the most part peopled, whose originals we pass by as having no form or comeliness. Assuredly the mission of every thinking man and woman is to help build up forms of greater beauty, spiritual, intellectual, material, everywhere; but if we would make something grander than Watteau gardens or Dresden china shepherdesses, we must enter the great realistic school of Nature and learn to recognize the beauty that already surrounds us, although it may have a little dirt on the surface. Then, when we have learnt the great principles of Beauty from the All-Spirit which is it, we shall know how to develop the Beauty on its own proper lines without perpetuating the dirt; and we shall know that all Beauty is the expression of Living Power, and that we can measure our power by the degree of beauty into which we can transform it, rendering our lives,

"By loveliness of perfect deeds,
More strong than all poetic thought."

Chapter XVI

Separation and Unity

I

"The prince of this world cometh, and hath nothing in Me" (John xiv, 30). In these words the Grand Master of Divine Science gives us the key to the Great Knowledge. Comparison with other passages shows that the terms here rendered "prince" and "world" can equally be rendered "principle" and "age." Jesus is here speaking of a principle of the present age so entirely opposed to that principle of which he himself was the visible expression, as to have no part in him. It is the utter contradiction of everything that Jesus came to teach and to exemplify. The account Jesus gave of himself was that he came "to bear witness to the Truth," and in order that men "might have life, and that they might have it more abundantly"; consequently the principle to which he refers must be the exact opposite of Truth and Life—that is, it must be the principle of Falsehood and Death.

What, then, is this false and destructive principle which rules the present age? If we consider the gist of the entire discourse of which these are the concluding words, we shall find that the central idea which Jesus has been most strenuously endeavoring to impress upon his disciples at their last meeting before the crucifixion, is that of the absolute identity and out-and-out oneness of "the Father" and "the Son," the principle of the perfect unity of God and Man. If this, then, was the great Truth which he was thus earnestly solicitous to impress upon his disciples' minds when his bodily presence was so shortly to be removed from them—the Truth of Unity—may we not reasonably infer the opposing falsehood to be the assertion of separateness, the assertion that God and man are not one? The idea of separateness is precisely the principle on which the world has proceeded from that day to this—the assumption that God and man are not one in being, and that the matter is of a different essence from spirit. In other words, the principle that finds favor with the intellectuality of the present age is that of duality—the idea of two powers and two substances opposite in kind, and, therefore, repugnant to each other, permeating all things, and so leaving no wholeness anywhere.

The entire object of the Bible is to combat the idea, of two opposing forces in the world. The good news is said to be that of "reconciliation" (2 Cor. v. 18), where also we are told that "all things are from God," hence leaving no room for any other power or any other substance; and the great falsehood, which it is the purpose of the Good News to expose, is everywhere in the Bible proclaimed to be the suggestion of duality, which is some other mode of Life, that is not the One Life, but something separate from it—an idea which it is impossible to state distinctly without involving a contradiction in terms. Everywhere the Bible exposes the fiction of the duality of separation as the great lie, but nowhere in so emphatic and concentrated a manner as in that wonderful passage of Revelations where it is figured in the mysterious Number of the Beast. "He that hath understanding let him count the number of the Beast ... and his number is six hundred and sixty and six" (Rev. xiii, 18, R.V.). Let me point out the great principle expressed in this mysterious number. It has other more particular applications, but this one general principle underlies them all.

It is an established maxim that every unity contains in itself a trinity, just as the individual man consists of body, soul, and spirit. If we would perfectly understand anything, we must be able to comprehend it in its threefold nature; therefore in symbolic numeration the multiplying of the unit by three implies the completeness of that for which the unit stands; and, again, the threefold repetition of a number represents its extension to infinity. Now mark what results if we apply these representative methods of numerical expression to the principles of Oneness and of separateness respectively. Oneness is Unity, and $1 \times 3 = 3$, which, intensified to its highest expression, is written as 333. Now apply the same method to the idea of separateness. Separateness consists of one and another one, each of which, according to the universal law, contains a trinity. In this view of duality the totality of things is two, and $2 \times 3 = 6$, and, intensifying this to its highest expression, we get 666, which is the Number of the Beast.

Why of the Beast? Because separateness from God, or the duality of opposition, which is also a duality of polarity, which is Dual-Unity, recognizes something as having essential being, which is not the One Spirit; and such a conception can be verbally rendered only by some word that in common acceptance represents something, not only lower than the divine, but lower than the human also. It is because the conception of oneself as a being apart from God, if carried out to its legitimate consequences, must ultimately land all who hold it in a condition of things where open ferocity or secret cunning, the tiger nature or the serpent nature, can be the only possible rule of action.

Thus it is that the principle of the present age can have no part in that principle of Perfect Wholeness which the Great Master embodied in His teaching and in Himself. The two ideas are absolutely incompatible, and whichever we adopt as our leading principle, it must be to the entire exclusion of the other; we cannot serve God and Mammon. There is no such thing as partial wholeness. Either we are still in the principle of Separateness, and our eyes are not yet open to the real nature of the Kingdom of Heaven; or else we have grasped the principle of Unity without any exception anywhere, and the

One Being includes all, the body and the soul alike, the visible form and the invisible substance and life of all equally; nothing can be left out, and we stand complete here and now, lacking no faculty, but requiring only to become conscious of our own powers, and to learn to have confidence in them through "having them exercised by reason of use."

The following communication from "A Foreign Reader," commenting on the Number of the Beast, as treated by Judge Troward in "Separation and Unity," is taken from *EXPRESSION* for 1902, in which it was first published. Following is Judge Troward's reply to this letter.

Dear Mr. Editor.—A correspondent in the current number of *Expression* points out the reference in the Book of Revelation to the number 666 as the mark of the Beast, because the trinity of mind, soul, and body, if considered as unity, may be expressed by the figures 333, and therefore duality is $333 \times 2 = 666$.

I think the inverse of the proposition is still more startling, and I should like to point it out. Instead of multiplying let us try dividing. First of all take unity as the unit one and divide by three (representing of course the same formula, viz., mind, soul and body). Expressed by a common fraction it is merely $1/3$, which is an incomplete mathematical figure. But take the decimal formula of one divided by three, and we arrive at .3 circulating, i. e., .3333 on to infinity. In other words, the result of the proposition by mathematics is that you divide this formula of spirit, soul, and body into unity, and it remains true to itself ad infinitum.

Now we come to consider it as a duality in the same way. Expressed as a vulgar fraction it is $2/3$; but as a decimal fraction it is .6666 ad infinitum. I think this is worth noting.

Yours very faithfully,
A Foreign Reader.

Brussels, Aug. 14, 1902.

Dear Editor.—I return with many thanks the very interesting letter received with yours, and I am very glad that my article should have been instrumental in drawing forth this further light on the subject.

This, moreover, affords an excellent illustration of one great principle of Unity, which is that the Unity repeats itself in every one of its parts, so that each part taken separately is an exact reproduction (in principles) of the greater Unity of which it is a portion. Therefore, if you take the individual man as your unit (which is what I did), and proceed by multiplication, you get the results which were pointed out in my article. And conversely, if you take the Great Unity of All-Being as your unit, and proceed by division, you arrive at the result shown by your foreign correspondent. The principle is a purely mathematical one, and is extremely interesting in the present application as showing the existence of a system of concealed mathematics running through the whole Bible. This bears out what I said in my article that there were other applications of the principle in question, though this one did not at the time occur to me.

I am much indebted to your correspondent for the further proof thus given of the correctness of my interpretation of the Number of the Beast. Both our interpretations support each other, for they are merely different ways of stating the same thing, and they have this advantage over those generally given, that they do not refer to any particular form of evil, but express a general principle applicable to all alike.

Yours sincerely,
T.
London, Aug. 30, 1902.

II

It may perhaps emphasize my point if I remind my readers that it was the conflict between the principles of Unity and separation that led to the crucifixion of Jesus. We must distinguish between the charge which really led to his death, and the merely technical charge on which he was sentenced by the Roman Governor. The latter—the charge of opposition to the royal authority of Cesar—has its significance; but it is clear from the Bible record that this was merely formal, the true cause of conviction being contained in the statement that of the chief priests: "We have a law, and by our law he ought to die, because he made himself the Son of God."

The antagonism of the two principles of Unity and separation had first been openly manifested on the occasion when Jesus made the memorable declaration, "I and my Father are one." The Jews took up stones to stone him. Then said Jesus unto them, "Many good works have I shown you from my Father; for which of those works do ye stone Me?" The Jews replied, "For a good work we stone thee not; but for blasphemy; and because that thou, being a man, makest thyself God." Jesus said, "Is it not written in your law, I said ye are gods? If He called them gods, unto whom the Word of God came (and the Scriptures cannot be broken), say ye of him, whom the Father hath sanctified, and sent into the world, thou blasphemest; because I said, I am the Son of God?" Here we have the first open passage of arms between the two opposing principles which led to the scene of Calvary as the final testimony of Jesus to the principle of Unity. He died because he maintained the Truth; that he was one with the Father. That was the substantive charge on which he was executed. "Art thou the son of the Blessed?" he was asked by the priestly tribunal; and the answer came clear and unequivocal, "I am." Then said the Council, "He hath spoken blasphemy, what further need have we of witnesses?" And they all condemned him to be worthy of death.

Jesus did not enter into a palpably useless argument with judges whose minds were so rooted in the idea of dualism as to be impervious to any other conception; but with a mixed multitude, who were not officially committed to a system, the case was different. Among them there might be some still open to conviction, and the appeal was, therefore, made to a passage in the Psalms with which they were all familiar, pointing out that the very persons to whom the Divine word was addressed were styled "gods" by the Divine Speaker Himself. The incontrovertibleness of the fact was emphasized by the stress laid upon it as "Scripture which cannot be broken;" and the meaning to be assigned to the statement was rendered clear by the argument which Jesus deduced from it. He says in effect, "You would stone me as a blasphemer for saying of myself what your own Scriptures say concerning each of you." The claim of unity with "the Father," he urges, was no unique one, but one which the Scripture, rightly understood, entitled every one of his hearers to make for himself.

And so we find throughout that Jesus nowhere makes any claim for himself which he does not also make for those who accept his teaching. Does he say to the Jews, "Ye are of this world; I am not of this world?" Equally he says of his disciples, "They are not of the world, even as I am not of the world." Does he say, "I am the light of the world?" Equally, he says, "Ye are the light of the world." Does he say, "I and my Father are one?" Equally he prays that they all might be one, even as we are one. Is he styled "the Son of God?" Then St. John writes, "To them gave he power to become sons of God, even to as many as believe on his name;" and by belief on the name we may surely understand belief in the principle of which the name is the verbal representation.

The essential unity of God and man is thus the one fact which permeates the whole teaching of Jesus. He himself stood forth as its living expression. He appealed to his miracles as the proofs of it: "it is the Father that doeth the works." It formed the substance of his final discourse with his disciples in the night that he was betrayed. It is the Truth, to bear witness to which, he told Pilate, was the purpose of his life. In support of this Truth he died, and by the living power of this Truth he rose again. The whole object of his mission was to teach men to realize their unity with God and the consequences that must necessarily follow from it; to draw them away from that notion of dualism which puts an impassable barrier between God and man, and thus renders any true conception of the Principle of Life impossible; and to draw them into the clear perception of the innermost nature of Life, as consisting in the inherent identity of each individual with that Infinite all-pervading Spirit of Life which he called "the Father."

"The branch cannot bear fruit except it abide in the vine;" the power of bearing fruit, of producing and of giving forth, depends entirely on the fact that the individual is, and always continues to be, as much an organic part of Universal Spirit as the fruit-bearing branch is an organic part of the parent stem. Lose this idea, and regard God as a merely external Creator who may indeed command us, or even sometimes be moved by our cries and entreaties, and we have lost the root of Livingness and with it all possibility of growth or of liberty. This is dualism, which cuts us off from our Source of Life; and so long as we take this false conception for the true law of Being, we shall find ourselves hampered by limitations and insoluble problems of every description: We have lost the Key of Life and are consequently unable to open the door.

But in proportion as we abide in the vine, that is, consciously realize our perpetual unity with Originating Spirit, and impress upon ourselves that this unity is neither bestowed as the reward of merit, nor as an act of favor—which would be to deny the Unity, for the bestowal would at once imply dualism—but dwell on the truth that it is the innermost and supreme principle of our own nature; in proportion as we consciously realize this, we shall rise to greater and greater certainty of knowledge, resulting in more and more perfect externalization, whose increasing splendor can know no limits; for it is the continual outflowing of the exhaustless Spirit of Life in that manifestation of itself which is our own individuality.

The notion of dualism is the veil which prevents men seeing this, and causes them to wander blindfolded among the mazes of endless perplexity; but, as St. Paul truly says, when this veil is taken away we shall find ourselves changed from glory to glory as by the Lord the Spirit. "His name shall be called Immanuel," that is "God *in* us," not a separate being from ourselves. Let us remember that Jesus was condemned by the principle of separation because he himself was the externalization of the principle of Unity, and that, in adhering to the principle of Unity we are adhering to the only possible root of Life, and are maintaining the Truth for which Jesus died.

Chapter XVII

Externalization

Who would not be happy in himself and his conditions? That is what we all desire—more fullness of life, a greater and brighter vitality in ourselves, and less restriction in our surroundings. And we are told that the talisman by which this can be accomplished is Thought. We are told, Change your modes of thought, and the changed conditions will follow. But many seekers feel that this is very much like telling us to catch birds by putting salt on their tails. If we can put the salt on the bird's tail, we can also lay our hand on the bird. If we can change our thinking, we can thereby change our circumstances.

But how are we to bring about this change of cause which will in its turn produce this changed effect? This is the practical question that perplexes many earnest seekers. They can see their way clearly enough through the whole sequence of cause and effect resulting in the externalization of the desired results, if only the one initial difficulty could be got over. The difficulty is a real one, and until it is overcome it vitiates all the teaching and reduces it to a mere paper theory. Therefore it is to this point that the attention of students should be particularly directed. They feel the need of some solid basis from which the change of thought can be effected, and until they find this the theory of Divine Science, however perfect in itself, will remain for them nothing more than a mere theory, producing no practical results.

The necessary scientific basis exists, however, and is extremely simple and reasonable, if we will take the pains to think it out carefully for ourselves. Unless we are prepared to support the thesis that the Power which created the universe is inherently evil, or that the universe is the work of two opposite and equal powers, one evil and the other good—both of which propositions are demonstrably false—we have no alternative but to say that the Originating Source of all must be inherently good. It cannot be partly good and partly evil, for that would be to set it against itself and make it self-destructive; therefore it must be good altogether. But once grant this initial proposition and we cut away the root of all evil. For how can evil proceed from an All-originating Source which is good altogether, and in which, therefore, no germ for the development of evil is to be found? Good cannot be the origin of evil; and since nothing can proceed except from the one Originating Mind, which is only good, the true nature of all things must be that which they have received from their Source—namely, good.

Hence it follows that evil is not the true nature of anything, and that evil must have its rise in something external to the true nature of things. And since evil is not in the true nature of the things themselves, nor yet in the Universal Mind which is the Originating Principle, there remains only one place for it to spring from, and that is our own personal thought. First we suppose evil to be as inherent in the nature of things as good—a supposition which we could not make if we stopped to consider the necessary nature of the Originating Principle. Then, on this entirely gratuitous supposition, we proceed to build up a fabric of fears, which, of course, follow logically from it; and so we nourish and give substance to the Negative, or that which has no substantial existence except such as we attribute to it, until we come to regard it as having Affirmative power of its own, and so set up a false idea of Being—the product of our own minds—to dispute the claims of true Being to the sovereignty of the universe.

Once assume the existence of two rival powers—one good and the other evil—in the direction of the universe, and any sense of harmony becomes impossible; the whole course of Nature is thrown out of gear, and, whether for ourselves or for the world at large, there remains no ground of certainty anywhere. And this is precisely the condition in which the majority of people live. They are surrounded by infinite uncertainty about everything, and are consequently a prey to continual fears and anxieties; and the only way of escape from this state of things is to go to the root of the matter, and realize that the whole fabric of evil originates in our own inverted conception of the nature of Being.

But if we once realize that the true conception of Being necessarily excludes the very idea of evil, we shall see that, in giving way to thoughts and fears of evil, we are giving substance to that which has no real substance in itself, and are attributing to the Negative an Affirmative force which it does not possess—in fact, we are creating the very thing we fear. And the remedy for this is always to recur to the original nature of Being as altogether Good, and then to speak to ourselves thus: "My thought must continually externalize something, for that is its inherent quality, which nothing can ever alter. Shall I, then, externalize God or the opposite of God? Which do I wish to see manifested in my life—Good or its opposite? Shall I manifest what I know to be the reality or the reverse?" Then comes the steady resolve always to manifest God, or Good, because that is the only true reality in all things; and this resolve is with power because it is founded upon the solid rock of Truth.

We must refuse to know evil; we must refuse to admit that there is any such thing to be known. It is the converse of this which is symbolized in the story of the Fall. "In the day that thou eatest thereof thou shalt surely die" was never spoken of the knowledge of Good, for Good never brought death into the world. It is eating the fruit of the tree of a so-called knowledge which admits a second branch, the knowledge of evil, that is the source of death. Admit that evil has a substantive entity, which renders it a subject of knowledge, and you thereby create it, with all its consequences of sorrow, sickness and death. But "be sure that the Lord He is God"—that is, that the one and Only Ruling Principle of the universe, whether within us or around us, is Good and Good only—and evil with all its train sinks back into its original nothingness, and we find that the Truth has made us free. We are free to externalize what we will, whether in ourselves or our surroundings, for we have found the solid basis on which to make the needed change of mental attitude in the fact that the Good is the only reality of Being.

1902.

Chapter XVIII

Entering into the Spirit of It

"Entering into the spirit of it." What a common expression! And yet how much it really means, how absolutely everything! We enter into the spirit of an undertaking, into the spirit of a movement, into the spirit of an author, even into the spirit of a game; and it makes all the difference both to us and to that into which we enter. A game without any spirit is a poor affair; and association in which there is no spirit falls to pieces; and a spiritless undertaking is sure to be a failure. On the other hand, the book which is meaningless to the unsympathising reader is full of life and suggestion to the one who enters into the spirit of the writer; the man who enters into the spirit of the music finds a spring of refreshment in some fine recital which is entirely missed by the cold critic who comes only to judge according to the standard of a rigid rule; and so on in every case that we can think of. If we do not enter the spirit of a thing, it has no invigorating effect upon us, and we regard it as dull, insipid and worthless. This is our everyday experience, and these are the words in which we express it. And the words are well chosen. They show our intuitive recognition of the spirit as the fundamental reality in everything, however small or however great. Let us be right as to the spirit of a thing, and everything else will successfully follow.

By entering into the spirit of anything we establish a mutual vivifying action and reaction between it and ourselves; we vivify it with our own vitality, and it vivifies us with a living interest which we call its spirit; and therefore the more fully we enter into the spirit of all with which we are concerned, the more thoroughly do we become *alive*. The more completely we do this the more we shall find that we are penetrating into the great secret of Life. It may seem a truism, but the great secret of Life is its Livingness, and it is just more of this quality of Livingness that we want to get hold of; it is that good thing of which we can never have too much.

But every fact implies also its negative, and we never properly understand a thing until we not only know what it is, but also clearly understand what it is not. To a complete understanding the knowledge of the negative is as necessary as the knowledge of the affirmative; for the perfect knowledge consists in realizing the relation between the two, and the perfect power grows out of this knowledge by enabling us to balance the affirmative and negative against each other in any proportion that we will, thus giving flexibility to what would otherwise be too rigid, and form to what would otherwise be too fluid; and so, by uniting these two extremes, to produce any result we may desire. It is the old Hermetic saying, "*Coagula et solve*"—"Solidify the fluid and dissolve the solid"; and therefore, if we would discover the secret of "entering into the spirit of it," we must get some idea of the negative, which is the "not-spirit."

In various ages this negative phase has been expressed in different forms of words suitable to the spirit of the time; and so, clothing this idea in the attire of the present day, I will sum up the opposite of Spirit in the word "Mechanism." Before all things this is a mechanical age, and it is astonishing how great a part of what we call our social advance has its root in the mechanical arts. Reduce the mechanical arts to what they were in the days of the Plantagenets and the greater part of our boasted civilization would recede through the centuries along with them. We may not be conscious of all this, but the mechanical tendency of the age has a firm grip upon society at large. We habitually look at the mechanical side of things by preference to any other. Everything is done mechanically, from the carving on a piece of furniture to the arrangement of the social system. It is the mechanism that must be considered first, and the spirit has to be fitted to the mechanical exigencies. We enter into the mechanism of it instead of into the Spirit of it, and so limit the Spirit and refuse to let it have its own way; and then, as a consequence, we get entirely mechanical action, and complete our circle of ignorance by supposing that this is the only sort of action there is.

Yet this is not a necessary state of things even in regard to "physical science," for the men who have made the greatest advances in that direction are those who have most clearly seen the subordination of the mechanical to the spiritual. The man who can recognize a natural law only as it operates through certain forms of mechanism with which he is familiar will never rise to the construction of the higher forms of mechanism which might be built up upon that law, for he fails to see that it is the law which determines the mechanism and not vice versa. This man will make no advance in science, either theoretical or applied, and the world will never owe any debt of gratitude to him. But the man who recognizes that the mechanism for the application of any principle grows out of the true apprehension of the principle studies the principle first, knowing that when *that* is properly grasped it will necessarily suggest all that is wanted for bringing it into practical use.

And if this is true in regard to so-called physical science, it is *a fortiori* true as regards the Science of Spirit. There is a mechanical attitude of mind which judges everything by the limitations of past experiences, allowing nothing for the fact that those experiences were for the most part the results of our ignorance of spiritual law. But if we realize the true law of Being we shall rise above these mechanical conceptions. We shall not deny the reality of the body or of the physical world as facts, knowing that they also are Spirit, but we shall learn to deny their power as causes. We shall learn to distinguish between the *causa causta* and the *causa causans*, the secondary or apparent physical cause and the primary or spiritual cause, without which the secondary cause could not exist; and so we shall get a new standpoint of clear knowledge and certain power by stepping over the threshold of the mechanical and entering into the spirit of it.

What we have to do is to maintain our even balance between the two extremes, denying neither Spirit nor the mechanism which is its form and through which it works. The one is as necessary to a perfect whole as the other, for there must be an *outside* as well as an *inside*; only we must remember that the creative principle is always *inside*, and that the outside only exhibits what the inside creates. Hence, whatever external effect we would produce, we must first enter into the spirit of it and work upon the spiritual principle, whether in ourselves or others; and by so doing our insight will become greatly enlarged, for from without we can see only one small portion of the circumference, while from the centre we can see the whole of it. If we fully grasp the truth that Spirit is Creator, we can dispense with painful investigations into the mechanical side of all our problems. If we are constructing from without, then we have to calculate anxiously the strength of our materials and the force of every thrust and strain to which they may be subjected, and very possibly after all we may find that we have made a mistake somewhere in our elaborate calculations. But if we realize the power of creating from within, we shall find all these calculations correctly made for us; for the same Spirit which is Creator is also that which the Bible calls "the Wonderful Numberer." Construction from without is based upon analysis, and no analysis is complete without accurate quantitative knowledge; but creation is the very opposite of analysis, and carries its own mathematics with it.

To enter into the spirit of anything, then, is to make yourself one in thought with the creative principle that is at the centre of it; and therefore why not go to the centre of all things at once, and enter into the Spirit of Life? Do you ask where to find it? *In yourself*; and in proportion as you find it there, you will find it everywhere else. Look at Life as the one thing that is, whether in you or around you; try to realize the livingness of it, and then seek to enter into the Spirit of it by affirming it to be the whole of what you are. Affirm this continually in your thoughts, and by degrees the affirmation will grow into a real living force within you, so that it will become a second nature to you, and you will find it impossible and unnatural to think in any other way; and the nearer you approach this point the greater you will find your control over both body and circumstances, until at last you shall so enter into the Spirit of it— into the Spirit of the Divine creative power which is the root of all things— that, in the words of Jesus, "nothing shall be impossible to you," because you have so entered into the Spirit of it that you discover yourself to be *one with it*. Then all the old limitations will have passed away, and you will be living in an entirely new world of Life, Liberty and Love, of which you yourself are the radiating centre. You will realize the truth that your Thought is a limitless creative power, and that you yourself are behind your Thought, controlling and directing it with Knowledge for any purpose which Love motives and Wisdom plans. Thus you will cease from your labors, your struggles and anxieties, and enter into that new order where perfect rest is one with ceaseless activity.

1902

Chapter XIX
The Bible and the New Thought

I
The Son

A deeply interesting subject to the student of the New Thought movement is to trace how exactly its teaching is endorsed by the teaching of the Bible. There is no such thing as new thought in the sense of new Truth, for what is truth now must have been truth always; but there is such a thing as a new presentment of the old Truth, and it is in this that the newness of the present movement consists. But the same Truth has been repeatedly stated in earlier ages under various forms and in various measures of completeness, and nowhere more completely than in the Scriptures of the Old and New Testaments. None of the older forms of statement is more familiarly known to our readers than that contained in the Bible, and no other is entwined around our hearts with the same sacred and tender associations: therefore, I have no hesitation in saying that the existence of a marked correspondence between its teaching and that of the New Thought cannot but be a source of strength and encouragement to any of us who have been accustomed in the past to look to the old and hallowed Book as a storehouse of Divine wisdom. We shall find that the clearer light will make the rough places smooth and the dim places luminous, and that of the treasures of knowledge hidden in the ancient volume the half has not been told us.

The Bible lays emphatic stress upon "the glorious liberty of the sons of God," thus uniting in a single phrase the twofold idea of filial dependence and personal liberty. A careful study of the subject will show us that there is no opposition between these two ideas, but that they are necessary correlatives to each other, and that whether stated after the more concentrated method of the Bible, or after the more detailed method of the New Thought, the true teaching proclaims, not our independence of God, but our independence in God.

Such an enquiry naturally centers in an especial manner around the sayings of Jesus; for whatever may be our opinions as to the nature of the authority with which he spoke, we must all agree that a peculiar weight attaches to those utterances which have come down to us as the *ipsissima verba* from which the entire New Testament has been developed; and if an identity of conception in the New Thought movement can be traced here at the fountain-head, we may expect to find it in the lower streams also.

The Key to the Master's teaching is to be found in his discourse with the Woman of Samaria, and it is contained in the statement that "the Father" is Spirit, that is, Spirit in the absolute and unqualified sense of the word, as appears from the original Greek, and not "A Spirit" as it is rendered in the Authorized Version: and then as the natural correlative to "the Father" we find another term employed, "the Son." The relation between these two forms the great subject of Jesus' teaching, and, therefore, it is most important to have some definite idea of what he meant by these terms if we would understand what it was that he really taught.

Now if "the Father" be Spirit, "the Son" must be Spirit also; for a son must necessarily be of the same nature as his father. But since "the Father" is Spirit, Absolute and Universal, it is evident that "the Son" cannot be Spirit, Absolute and Universal, because there cannot be two Universal Spirits, for then neither would be universal. We may, therefore, logically infer that because "the Father" is Universal Spirit, "the Son" is Spirit not universal; and the only definition of Spirit not-universal is Spirit individualized and particular. The Scripture tells us that "the Spirit is Life," and taking this as the definition of "Spirit," we find that "the Father" is Absolute, Originating, Undifferentiated Life, and "the Son" is the same Life differentiated into particular forms. Hence, in the widest sense of the expression, "the Son" stands for the whole creation, visible or invisible, and in this sense it is the mere differentiation of the universal Life into a multiplicity of particular modes. But if we have any adequate idea of the intelligent and responsive nature of Spirit [1] —if we realize that because it is Pure Being it must be Infinite Intelligence and Infinite Responsiveness—then we shall see that its reproduction in the particular admits of innumerable degrees, from mere expression as outward form up to

---

[1] *Intelligence* and *Responsiveness* is the Generic Nature of Spirit in *every* Mode, and it is the *concentration* of this into centers of consciousness that makes personality, i. e., *self*-conscious individuality. This varies immensely in degree, from its first adumbration in the animal to its intense development in the Great Masters of Spiritual Science. Therefore it is called "The Power that Knows Itself"—It is the power of *Self*-recognition that makes *personality*, and as we grow to see that our personality is not all contained between our hat and our boots, as Walt Whitman says, but *expands* away into the Infinite, which we then find to be *the Infinite of ourselves*, the *same* I AM that I am, so *our personality* expands and we become conscious of ever-increasing degrees of Life-in-ourselves.

the very fullest expression of the infinite intelligence and responsiveness that Spirit is.

The teachings of Jesus were addressed to the hearts and intelligences of men, and therefore the grade of sonship of which he spoke has reference to the expression of Infinite Being in the human heart and intellect. But this, again, may be conceived of in infinite degrees; in some men there is the bare potentiality of sonship entirely undeveloped as yet, in others the beginnings of its development, in others a fuller development, and so on, until we can suppose some supreme instance in which the absolutely perfect reproduction of the universal has been attained. Each of these stages constitutes a fuller and fuller expression of sonship, until the supreme development reaches a point at which it can be described only as the perfect image of "the Father"; and this is the logical result of a process of steady growth from an inward principle of Life which constitutes the identity of each individual.

It is thus a necessary inference from Jesus' own explanation of "the Father" as Spirit or Infinite Being that "the Son" is the Scriptural phrase for the reproduction of Infinite Being in the individual, contemplated in that stage at which the individual does in some measure begin to recognize his identity with his originating source, or, at any rate, where he has capacity for such a recognition, even though the actual recognition may not yet have taken place. It is very remarkable that, thus defining "the Son" on the direct statement of Jesus himself, we arrive exactly at the definition of Spirit as "that power which knows itself." In the capacity for thus recognizing its identity of nature with "the Father" is it that the potential fact of sonship consists, for the prodigal son was still a son even before he began to realize his relation to his "Father" in actual fact. It is the dawning of this recognition that constitutes the spiritual "babe," or infant son; and by degrees this consciousness grows till he attains the full estate of spiritual manhood. This recognition by the individual of his own identity with Universal Spirit is precisely what forms the basis of the New Thought; and thus at the outset the two systems radiate from a common centre.

But I suppose the feature of the New Thought which is the greatest stumbling-block to those who view the movement from the outside is the claim it makes for Thought-power as an active factor in the affairs of daily life. As a mere set of speculative opinions people might be willing to pigeon-hole it along with the philosophic systems of Kant or Hegel; but it is the practical element in it which causes the difficulty. It is not only a system of Thought based upon a conception of the Unity of Being, but it claims to follow out this conception to its legitimate consequences in the production of visible and tangible external results by the mere exercise of Thought-power. A ridiculous claim, a claim not to be tolerated by common sense, a trespassing upon the Divine prerogative, a claim of unparalleled audacity: thus the casual objector. But this claim is not without its parallel, for the same claim was put forward on the same ground by the Great Teacher Himself as the proper result of "the Son's" recognition of his relation to "the Father." "Ask what ye will, and it shall be done unto you"; "Whatsoever you shall ask in prayer, believing, you shall receive, and nothing shall be impossible unto you"; "All things are possible to him that believeth." These statements are absolutely without any note of limitation save that imposed by the seeker's want of faith in his own power to move the Infinite. This is as clear a declaration of the efficacy of mental power to produce outward and tangible results as any now made by the New Thought, and it is made on precisely the same ground, namely, the readiness of "the Father" or Spirit in the Universal to respond to the movement of Spirit in the individual.

In the Bible this movement of individualized Spirit is called "prayer," and it is synonymous with Thought, formulated with the intention of producing this response.

"Prayer is the heart's sincere desire, Uttered or unexpressed,"

and we must not let ourselves be misled by the association of particular forms with particular words, but should follow the sound advice of Oliver Wendell Holmes, and submit such words to a process of depolarization, which brings out their real meaning. Whether we call our act "prayer" or "thought-concentration," we mean the same thing; it is the claim of the man to move the Infinite by the action of his own mind.

It may be objected, however, that this definition omits an important element of prayer, the question, namely, whether God will hear it. But this is the very element that Jesus most rigorously excludes from his description of the mental act. Prayer, according to the popular notion, is a most uncertain matter. Whether we shall be heard or not depends entirely upon another will, regarding whose action we are completely ignorant, and therefore, according to this notion, the very essence of prayer consists of utter uncertainty. Jesus' conception of prayer was the very opposite. He bids us believe that we have already in fact received what we ask for, and makes this the condition of receiving; in other words, he makes the essential factor in the mental action to consist in Absolute Certainty as to the corresponding response in the Infinite, which is exactly the condition that the New Thought lays down for the successful operation of Thought-power.

It may, however, be objected that if men have thus an indiscriminate power of projecting their thought to the accomplishment of anything they desire, they can do so for evil as easily as for good. But Jesus fully recognized this possibility, and worked the only destructive miracle recorded of him for the express purpose of emphasizing the danger. The reason given by the compilers of the Gospel for the destruction of the fig-tree is clearly inadequate, for we certainly cannot suppose Jesus so unreasonable as to curse a tree for not bearing fruit out of season. But the record itself shows a very different purpose. Jesus answered the disciples' astonished questioning by telling them that it was in their own power, not only to do what was done to the fig-tree, but to produce effects upon a far grander scale; and he concludes the conversation by laying down the duty of a heart-searching forgiveness as a necessary preliminary to prayer. Why was this precept so particularly impressed in this particular connection? Obviously because the demonstration he had just given of the valency of thought-power in the hands of instructed persons laid bare the fact that this power can be used destructively as well as beneficially, and that, therefore, a thorough heart-searching for the eradication of any lurking ill-feeling became an imperative preliminary to its safe use; otherwise there was danger of noxious thought-currents being set in motion to the injury of others. The miracle of the fig-tree was an object-lesson to exhibit the need for the careful handling of that limitless power which Jesus assured his disciples existed as fully in them as in himself. I do not here attempt to go into this subject in detail, but enough has, I think, been shown to convince us that Jesus made exactly the same claim for the power of Thought as that made by the New Thought movement at the present day. It is a great claim, and it is, therefore, encouraging to find such an authority committed to the same assertion.

The general principle on which this claim is based by the exponents of the New Thought is the identity of Spirit in the individual with spirit in the universal, and we shall find that this, also, is the basis of Jesus' teaching on the subject. He says that "the Son can do nothing of himself, but what he seeth the Father do these things doeth the Son in like manner." It must now be sufficiently clear that "the Son" is a generic appellation, not restricted to a particular individual, but applicable to all; and this statement explains the manner of "the Son's" working in relation to "the Father." The point this sentence particularly emphasizes is that it is what he sees the Father doing that the Son does also. His doing corresponds to his seeing. If the seeing expands, the doing expands along with it. But we are all sufficiently familiar with this principle in other matters. What differentiates an Edison or a Marconi from the apprentice who knows only how to fit up an electric bell by rule of thumb? It is their capacity for seeing the universal principles of electricity and bringing them into particular application. The great painter is the one who sees the universal principles of form and color where the smaller man sees only a particular combination; and so with the great surgeon, the great chemist, the great lawyer—in every line it is the power of insight that distinguishes the great man from the little one; it is the capacity for making wide generalizations and perceiving far-reaching laws that raises the exceptional mind above the ordinary level. The greater working always results from the greater seeing into the abstract principles from which any art or science is generated; and this same law carried up to the universal principles of Life is the law by which "the Son's" working is proportioned to his seeing the method of "the Father's" work. Thus the source of "the Son's" power lies in the contemplation of "the Father," the Endeavour, that is, to realize the true nature of Being, whether in the abstract or in its generic forms of manifestation. [2]This is Bacon's maxim, "Work as God works"; and similarly the New Thought consists before all things in the realization of the laws of Being.

And the result of the seeing is that "the Son" does the same things as "the Father" "in like manner." The Son's action is the reproduction of the universal principles in application to specific instances. The principles remain unaltered and work always in the same manner, and the office of "the Son" is to determine the particular field of their operation with regard to the specific object which he has in view; and therefore, so far as that object is concerned, the action of "the Son" becomes the action of "the Father" also.

Again, there is no concealment on the part of "the Father." He has no secrets, for "the Father loveth the Son, and showeth him all things that himself doeth." There is perfect reciprocity between Spirit in the Universal and in Individualization, resulting from the identity of Being; and "the Son's" recognition of Love as the active principle of this Unity gives him an intuitive insight into all those inner workings of the Universal Life which we call the arcana of Nature. Love has a divine gift of insight which cannot be attained by intellect alone, and the old saying, "Love will find out the way," has greater depths of meaning than appear on the surface. Thus there is not only a seeing, but also a showing; and the three terms—"looking, seeing, showing"—combine to form a power of "working" to which it is impossible to assign any limit.

---

[2] Everything depends on this principle of Reciprocity. By contemplation we come to realize the true nature of "Spirit" or "the father." We learn to disengage the *variable* factors of particular *Modes* from the *invariable* factors which are the essential qualities of Spirit underlying *all* Modes. Then when we realize these essential qualities we see that we can apply them under any mode that we will: in other words *we* supply the *variable* factor of the combination by the action of our Thought, as Desire or Will, and thus combine it with the *invariable* factor or "constant" of the *essential* law of spirit, thus producing what result we will. This is just what we do in respect to physical nature—e. g., the electrician supplies the *variable* factor of the particular Mode of application, and the *constant* laws of Electricity *respond* to the nature of the invitation given to them. This *Responsiveness* is *inherent* in Spirit; otherwise Spirit would have no means of expansion into manifestation. Responsiveness is the principle of Spirit's Self-expression. We do not have to create responsive action on the part of electricity. We can safely take this Responsiveness for granted as pure natural law. Our desire first works on the Arupa level and thence concentrates itself through the various Rupa levels till it reaches complete external manifestation.

Here, again, the teaching of Jesus is in exact correspondence with that of the New Thought, which tells us that limitations exist only where we ourselves put them, and that to view ourselves as beings of limitless knowledge, power, and love is to become such in outward manifestation of visible fact. Any objection, therefore, to the New Thought teaching regarding the possibilities latent in Man apply with equal force to the teachings of Jesus. His teaching clearly was that the perfect individuality of Man is a Dual-Unity, the polarization of the Infinite in the Manifest; and it requires only the recognition of this truth for the manifested element in this binary system to demonstrate its identity with the corresponding element which is not externally visible. He said that He and his Father were One, that those who had seen him had seen the Father, that the words which he spoke were the Father's, and that it was the Father who did the works. Nothing could be more explicit. Absolute unity of the manifested individuality with the Originating Infinite Spirit is asserted or implied in every utterance attributed to Jesus, whether spoken of himself or of others. He recognizes only one radical difference, the difference between those who know this truth and those who do not know it. The distinction between the disciple and the master is one only of degree, which will be effaced by the expansive power of growth; "the disciple, when he is perfected, shall be as his Master."

All that hinders the individual from exercising the full power of the Infinite for any purpose whatever is his lack of faith, his inability to realize to the full the stupendous truth that he himself is the very power which he seeks. This was the teaching of Jesus as it is that of the New Thought; and this truth of the Divine Sonship of Man once taken as the great foundation, a magnificent edifice of possibilities which "eye hath not seen, nor ear heard, neither hath entered into the heart of man to conceive," grows up logically upon it—a glorious heritage which each one may legitimately claim in right of his common humanity.

II
The Great Affirmation

I take it for granted that my readers are well acquainted with the part assigned to the principle of Affirmation in the scheme of the New Thought. This is often a stumbling-block to beginners; and I feel sure that even those who are not beginners will welcome every aid to a deeper apprehension of this great central truth. I, therefore, purpose to examine the Bible teaching on this important subject.

The professed object of the Bible is to establish and extend "the Kingdom of God" throughout the world, and this can be done only by repeating the process from one individual to another, until the whole mass is leavened. It is thus an individual process; and, as we have seen in the last chapter, God is Spirit and Spirit is Life, and, therefore, the expansion of "the Kingdom of God" means the expansion of the principle of Life in each individual. Now Life, to be life at all, must be Affirmative. It is Life in virtue of what it is, and not in virtue of what it is not. The quantity of life in any particular case may be very small; but, however small the amount, the quality is always the same: it is the quality of Being, the quality of Livingness, and not its absence, that makes it what it is. The distinctive character of Life, therefore, is that it is Positive and not Negative; and every degree of negativeness, that is, every limitation, is ultimately traceable to deficiency of Life-power.

Limitations surround us because we believe in our inability to do what we desire. Whenever we say "I cannot" we are brought up sharp by a limitation, and we cease to exercise our thought-power in that direction because we believe ourselves stopped by a blank wall of impossibility; and whenever this occurs we are subjected to bondage. The ideal of perfect Liberty is the converse of all this, and follows a sequence which does not thus lead us into a *cul-de-sac*. This sequence consists of the three affirmations: I am—therefore I can—therefore I will; and this last affirmation results in the projection of our powers, whether interior or external, to the accomplishment of the desired object. But this last affirmation has its root in the first; and it is because we recognize the Affirmative nature of the Life that is in us, or rather of the Life which we are, that the power to will or to act positively has any existence; and, therefore, the extent of our power to will and to act positively and with effect, is exactly measured by our perception of the depth and livingness of our own Being. Hence the more fully we learn to affirm that, the greater power we are able to exercise.

Now the ideal of perfect Liberty is the entire absence of all limitation, and to have no limitation in Being is to be co-extensive with All-Being. We are all grammarians enough to know that the use of a predicate is to lead the mind to contemplate the subject as represented by that predicate; in other words, it limits our conception for the time being to that particular aspect of the subject. Hence every predicate, however extensive, implies some limitation of the subject. But the ideal subject, the absolutely free self, is, by the very hypothesis, without limitation; and, therefore, no predicate can be attached to it. It stands as a declaration of its own Being without any statement of what that Being consists in, and therefore it says of itself, not "I am this or that," but simply I am. No predicate can be added, because the only commensurate predicate would be the enumeration of Infinity. Therefore, both logically and grammatically, the only possible statement of a fully liberated being is made in the words I am.

I need hardly remind my readers of the frequency with which Jesus employed these emphatic words. In many cases the translators have added the word "He," but they have been careful, by putting it in italics, to show that it is not in the original. As grammarians and theologians they thought something more was wanted to complete the sense, and they supplied it accordingly; but if we would get at the very words as the Master himself spoke them, we must strike out this interpolation. And as soon as we have done so there flashes into light the identity of his statement with that made to Moses at the burning bush, where the full significance of the words is so obvious that the translators were compelled to leave the place of the predicate in that seeming emptiness which comes from filling all things.

Seen thus, a marvelous light shines forth from the instruction of the Great Teacher: for in whatever sense we may regard him as a Great Exception to the weak and limited aspect of humanity with which we are only too familiar, we must all agree that his mission was not to render mankind hopeless by declaring the path of advance barred against them, but "to give light to them that sit in darkness," and liberty to them that are bound, by proclaiming the unlimited possibilities that are in man waiting only to be called forth by knowledge of the Truth. And if we suppose any personal reference in his words, it can, therefore, be only as the Great Example of what man has it in him to become, and not as the example of something which man can never hope to be; an Exception, truly, to mankind as we see them now, but the Exception that proves the rule, and sets the standard of what each one may become as he attains to the measure of the stature of the fullness of Christ.

Let us, therefore, by striking out this interpolation, restore the Master's words as they stand in the original: "Except ye believe that I am, ye shall die in your sins." This is an epitome of his teaching.

"The last enemy that shall be overcome is death," and the "sting," or fatal power, of death is "sin." Remove that, and death has no longer any dominion over us; its power is at an end. And "the strength of sin is the Law": sin is every contradiction of the law of Being; and the law of Being is infinitude; for Being is Life, and Life in its innermost essence is the limitless I am. Dying in our sins is thus not a punishment for doubting a particular theological dogma, but it is the unavoidable natural consequence of not realizing, not believing in, the I am. So long as we fail to realize its full infinitude in ourselves, we cut ourselves off from our conscious unity with the Infinite Life-Spirit which permeates all things. Without this principle we have no alternative but to die—and this because of our sin, that is, because of our failure to conform to the true Law of our Being, which is Life, and not Death. We affirm Death and Negation concerning ourselves, and therefore Death and Negation are externalized, and thus we pay the penalty of not believing in the central Law of our own Life, which is the Law of all Life. The Bible is the Book of Principles, and therefore by "dying" is meant the acceptance of the principle of the Negative which culminates in Death as the sum-total of all limitations, and which introduces at every step those restrictions which are of the nature of Death, because their tendency is to curtail the outflowing fullness of Life.

This, then, is the very essence of the teaching of Jesus, that unbelief in the limitless power of Life-in-ourselves—in each of us—is the one cause of Death and of all those evils which, in greater or lesser measure, reproduce the restrictive influences which deprive Life of its fullness and joy. If we would escape Death and enter into Life, we must each believe in the I am in ourselves. And the ground for this belief? Simply that nothing else is conceivable. If our life is not a portion of the life of Universal Spirit, whence comes it? We are because that is. No other explanation is possible. The unqualified affirmation of our own livingness is not an audacious self-assertion: it is the only logical outcome of the fact that there is any life anywhere, and that we are here to think about it. In the sense of Universal Being, there can be only One I am, and the understanding use of the words by the individual is the assertion of this fact. The forms of manifestation are infinite, but the Life which is manifested is One, and thus every thinker who recognizes the truth regarding himself finds in the I am both himself and the totality of all things; and thus he comes to know that in utilizing the interior nature of the things and persons about him, he is, in effect, employing the powers of his own life.

Sometimes the veil which Jesus drew over this great truth was very transparent. To the Samaritan woman he spoke of it as a spring of Life forever welling up in the innermost recesses of man's being; and again, to the multitude assembled at the Temple, he spoke of it as a river of Life forever gushing from the secret sources of the spirit within us. Life, to be ours at all, must be ourselves. An energy which only passed through us, without being us, might produce a sort of galvanic activity, but it would not be Life. Life can never be a separate entity from the individuality which manifests it; and therefore, even if we conceive the life-principle in a man so intensified as to pulsate with what might seem to us an absolutely divine vitality, it would still be no other than the man himself. Thus Jesus directs us to no external source of life, but ever teaches that the Kingdom of Heaven is within, and that what is wanted is to remove those barriers of ignorance and ill-will which prevent us from realizing that the great I am, which is the innermost Spirit of Life throughout the universe, is the same I am that I am, whoever I may be.

On another memorable occasion Jesus declared again that the I am is the enduring principle of Life. It is this that is the Resurrection and the Life; not, as Martha supposed, a new principle to be infused from without at some future time, but an inherent core of vitality awaiting only its own recognition of itself to triumph over death and the grave. And yet, again hear the Master's answer to the inquiring Thomas. How many of us, like him, desire to know the way! To hear of wonderful powers latent in man and requiring only development is beautiful and hopeful, if we could only find out the way to develop them; but who will show us the way? The answer comes with no uncertain note. The I am includes everything. It is at once "the Way, the Truth, and the Life": not the Life only, or the Truth only, but also the Way by which to reach them. Can words be plainer? It is by continually affirming and relying on the I am in ourselves as identical with the I am that is the One and Only Life, whether manifested or unmanifested, in all places of the universe, that we shall find the way to the attainment of all Truth and of all Life. Here we have the predicate which we are seeking to complete our affirmation regarding ourselves. I am—what? the Three things which include all things: Truth, which is all Knowledge and Wisdom; Life, which is all Power and Love; and the unfailing Way which will lead us step by step, if we follow it, to heights too sublime and environment too wide for our present juvenile imaginings to picture.

As the New Testament centers around Jesus, so the old Testament centers around Moses, and he also declares the Great Affirmation to be the same. 3For

---

3 The Old Testament and the New treat the I AM from its opposite poles. The Old Testament treats it from the relation of the *Whole to the Part*, while the New Testament treats it from the relation of the *Part to the Whole*. This is important as explaining the relation between the Old and New Testaments.

(a) "My Word shall not return unto me void but shall accomplish that whereunto I send it."

(b) The Principle here indicated is that of the Alternation and Equation between Absorption and Radiation—a taking-in before, and a giving-out.

(c) "*Order*"—Whatever betrays this is "Disorder."

(d) "*Conscious*"—It is the degree of *consciousness* that always marks the transition from a lower to a higher Power of Life. The *Life* of *All Seven* Principles *must* always be present in us, otherwise we should not exist at all; therefore it is the degree in which we learn to *consciously* function in each of them that marks our advance into higher kingdoms within ourselves, and frequently outside ourselves also.

(e) The Central Radiating Point of our Individuality is *One* with All-Being.

(f) *Equilibrium*—Note the difference between the Living Equilibrium of Alternate Rhythmic *Pulsation* (the whole Pulsation Doctrine) and the dead equilibrium of merely *running down* to a *dead level*. The former implies the Doctrine of the Return, the Upward Arc compensating the Downward Arc—The deadness of the latter results from the absence him God has no name, but that intensely living universal Life which is all in all, and no name is sufficient to be its equivalent. The emphatic words I am are the only possible statement of the One-Power which exhibits itself as all worlds and all living beings. It is the Great I am which forever unfolds itself in all the infinite evolutionary forces of the cosmic scheme, and which, in marvelous onward march, develops itself into higher and higher conscious intelligence in the successive races of mankind, unrolling the scroll of history as it moves on from age to age, working out with unerring precision the steady forward movement of the whole towards that ultimate perfection in which the work of God will be completed. But stupendous as is the scale on which this Providential Power reveals itself to Moses and the Prophets, it is still nothing else than the very same Power which Jesus bids us realize in ourselves.

The theatre of its operations may be expanded to the magnificent proportions of a world-history, or contracted to the sphere of a single individuality: the difference is only one of scale; but the Life-principle is always the same. It is always the principle of confident Affirmation in the calm knowledge that all things are but manifestations of itself, and that, therefore, all must move together in one mighty unity which admits of no discordant elements. This "unity of the spirit" once clearly grasped, to say I am is to send the vibrations of our thought-currents throughout the universe to do our bidding when and where we will; and, conversely, it is *to* draw in the vitalizing influences of Infinite Spirit as from a boundless ocean of Life, which can never be exhausted and from which no power can hold us back. And all this is so because it is the supreme law of Nature. It is not the introduction of a new order, but simply the allowing of the original and only possible order to flow on to its legitimate fulfillment. A Divine Order, truly, but nowhere shall we find anything that is not Divine; and it is to the realization of this Divine and Living Order that it is the purpose of the Bible to lead us. But we shall never realize it around us until we first realize it within us. We can see God outside only by the light of God inside; and this light increases in proportion as we become conscious of the Divine nature of the innermost I am which is the centre of our own individuality.

---

of any such compensation. The Upward Arc results from the contemplation of the Highest Ideal.

(g) Spirit cannot leave any portion of its Nature behind it. It *must* always have *all* the qualities of Spirit in it, even though the lower parts of the individuality are not yet conscious of it.

(h) The Great Affirmation is The Guide to the whole Subject.

Therefore, it is that Jesus tells us that the I am is "the door." It is that central point of our individual Being which opens into the whole illimitable Life of the Infinite. If we would understand the old-world precept, "know thyself," we must concentrate our thought more and more closely upon our own interior Life until we touch its central radiating point, and there we shall find that the door into the Infinite is indeed opened to us, and that we can pass from the innermost of our own Being into the innermost of All-Being. This is why Jesus spoke of "the door" as that through which we should pass in and out and find pasture. Pasture, the feeding of every faculty with its proper food, is to be found both on the within and the without. The livingness of Life consists in both concentration and externalization: it is not the dead equilibrium of inertia, but the living equilibrium of a vital and rhythmic pulsation. Involution and evolution must forever alternate, and the door of communication between them is the I am which is the living power in both. Thus it is that the Great Affirmation is the Secret of Life, and that to say I am with a true understanding of all that it implies is to place ourselves in touch with all the powers of the Infinite.

This is the Universal and Eternal Affirmation to which no predicate is attached; and all particular affirmations will be found to be only special differentiations of this all-embracing one. I will this or that particular thing because I know that I can bring it into externalization, and I know that I can because I know that I am, and so we always come back to the great central Affirmation of All-Being. Search the Scriptures and you will find that from first to last they teach only this: that every human soul is an individualization of that Universal Being, or All-Spirit, which we call God, and that Spirit can never be shorn of its powers, but like Fire, which is its symbol, must always be fully and perfectly itself, which is Life in all its unlimited fullness.

In assigning to Affirmation, therefore, the importance which it does, the New Thought movement is at one with the teaching of Jesus and Moses and of the entire Bible. And the reason is clear. There is only one Truth, and therefore careful seeking can bring men only to the same Truth, whether they be Bible-writers or any other. The Bible derives its authority from the inherent truth of the things it tells of, and not vice versa; and if these things be true at all, they would be equally true even though no Bible had ever been written. But, taking the Great Affirmation as our guide, we shall find that the system taught by the Bible is scientific and logical throughout, and therefore any other system which is scientifically true will be found to correspond with it in substance, however it may differ from it in form; and thus, in their statements regarding the power of Affirmation, the exponents of the New Thought broach no new-fangled absurdity, but only reiterate a great truth which has been before the world, though very imperfectly recognized, for thousands of years.

III
The Father

If, as we have seen, "the Son" is the differentiating principle of Spirit, giving rise to innumerable individualities, "the Father" is the unifying principle by which these innumerable individualities are bound together into one common life, and the necessity for recognizing this great basis of the universal harmony forms the foundation of Jesus' teaching on the subject of Worship. "Woman, believe me, the hour cometh, when neither in this mountain, nor yet at Jerusalem, shall ye worship the Father. Ye worship that which ye know not; we worship that which we know; for salvation is from the Jews. But the hour cometh and now is when the true worshippers shall worship the Father in spirit and truth" (Revised Version). In these few words the Great Teacher sums up the whole subject. He lays particular stress on the kind of worship that he means. It is, before all things, founded upon knowledge.

"We worship that which we know," and it is this knowledge that gives the worship a healthful and life-giving quality. It is not the ignorant worship of wonderment and fear, a mere abasement of ourselves before some vast, vague, unknown power, which may injure us if we do not find out how to propitiate it; but it is a definite act performed with a definite purpose, which means that it is the employment of one of our natural faculties upon its proper object in an intelligent manner. The ignorant Samaritan worship is better than no worship at all, for at least it realizes the existence of some centre around which a man's life should revolve, something to prevent the aimless dispersion of His powers for want of a centripetal force to bind them together; and even the crudest notion of prayer, as a mere attempt to induce God to change his mind, is at least a first step towards the truth that full supply for all our needs may be drawn from the Infinite. Still, such worship as this is hampered with perplexities, and can give only a feeble answer to the atheistical sneer which asks, "What is man, that God should be mindful of him, a momentary atom among unnumbered worlds?"

Now the teaching of Jesus throws all these perplexities aside with the single word "knowledge." There is only one true way of doing anything, and that is knowing exactly what it is we want to do, and knowing exactly why we want to do it. All other doing is blundering. We may blunder into the right thing sometimes, but we cannot make this our principle of life to all eternity; and if we have to give up the blunder method eventually, why not give it up now, and begin at once to profit by acting according to intelligible principle? The knowledge that "the Son," as individualized Spirit, has his correlative in "the Father," as Universal Spirit, affords the clue we need.

In whatever way we may attempt to explain it, the fact remains that volition is the fundamental characteristic of Spirit. We may speak of conscious, or subconscious or super-conscious action; but in whatever way we may picture to ourselves the condition of the agent as contemplating his own action, a general purposeful lifeward tendency becomes abundantly evident on any enlarged view of Nature, whether seen from without or from within, and we may call this by the general name of volition. But the error we have to avoid is that of supposing volition to take the same form in Universal Spirit as in individualized Spirit. The very terms "universal" and "individual" forbid this. For the universal, as such, to exercise specific volition, concentrating itself upon the details of a specific case, would be for it to pass into individualization, and to cease to be the Absolute and Infinite; it would be no longer "the Father," but "the Son." It is therefore exactly by not exercising specific volition that "the Father" continues to be "the Father," or the Great Unifying Principle. But the volitional quality is not on this account absent from Spirit in the Universal; for otherwise whence would that quality appear in ourselves? It is present; but according to the nature of the plane on which it is acting. The Universal is not the Specific, and everything on the plane of the Universal must partake of the nature of that plane. Hence volition in "the Father" is not specific; and that which is not specific and individual must be generic. Generic volition, therefore, is that mode of volition which belongs to the Universal, and generic volition is tendency. This is the solution of the enigma, and this solution is given, not obscurely, in Jesus' statement that "the Father" seeks those true worshippers who worship Him in spirit and in truth.

For what do we mean by tendency? From the root of tendere, to stretch; it signifies a pushing out in a certain definite direction, the tension of some force seeking to expand itself. What force? The Universal Life-Principle, for "the Spirit is Life." In the language of modern science this "seeking" on the part of "the Father" is the expansive pressure of the Universal Life-Principle seeking the line of least resistance, along which to flow into the fullest manifestation of individualized Life. It is a tendency which will take manifested form according to the degree in which it meets with reception.

St. John says, "This is the boldness that we have towards him, that if we ask anything according to His will, He heareth us; and if we know that He heareth us whatsoever we ask, we know that we have the petitions that we have asked of Him" (1 John v. 14). Now according to the popular notion of "the will of God," this passage entirely loses its value, because it makes everything depend on our asking "according to His will," and if we start with the idea of an individual act of the Divine volition in each separate case, nothing short of a special revelation continually repeated could inform us what the Divine will in each particular instance was. Viewed in this light, this passage is a mere jeering at our incapacity. But when once we realize that "the will of God" is an invariable law of tendency, we have a clear standard by which to test whether we may rightly expect to get what we desire. We can study this law of tendency as we would any other law, and it is this study that is the essence of true worship.

The word "worship" means to count worthy; to count worthy, that is, of observation. The proverb says that "imitation is the sincerest form of flattery" more truly we may say that it is the sincerest worship. Hence the true worship is the study of the Universal Life-Principle "the Father," in its nature and in its modes of action; and when we have thus realized "the Law of God," the law that is inherent in the nature of Infinite Being, we shall know that by conforming our own particular action to this generic law, we shall find that this law will in every instance work out the results that we desire. This is nothing more or less miraculous than what occurs in every case of applied science. He only is the true chemist or engineer who, by first learning how to obey the generic tendency of natural laws, is able to command them to the fulfillment of his individual purposes; no other method will succeed. Similarly with the student of the divine mystery of Life. He must first learn the great laws of its generic tendency, and then he will be in a position to apply that tendency to the working of any specific effect he will.

Common sense tells us what the law of this tendency must be. The Master taught that a house divided against itself cannot stand; and for the Life-Principle to do anything restrictive of the fullest expansion of life, would be for it to act to its own destruction. The test, therefore, in every case, whether our intention falls within the scope of the great law, is this: Does it operate for the expansion or for the restriction of life? and according to the answer we can say positively whether or not our purpose is according to "the will of God." Therefore so long as we work within the scope of this generic "will of the Father" we need have no fear of the Divine Providence, as an agency, acting adversely to us. We may dismiss this bugbear, for we ourselves are manifestations of the very power which we call "the Father." The I am is one; and so long as we preserve this unity by conforming to the generic nature of the I am in the universal, it will certainly never destroy the unity by entering upon a specific course of action on its own account.

Here, then, we find the secret of power. It is contained in the true worship of "the Father," which is the constant recognition of the lifegivingness of Originating Spirit, and of the fact that we, as individuals, still continue to be portions of that Spirit; and that therefore the law of our nature is to be perpetually drawing life from the inexhaustible stores of the Infinite—not bottles of water-of-life mixed with other ingredients and labeled for this or that particular purpose, but the full flow of the pure stream itself, which we are free to use for any purpose we desire. "Whosoever will, let him take the water of life freely." It is thus that the worship of "the Father" becomes the central principle of the individual life, not as curtailing our liberty, but as affording the only possible basis for it. As a planetary system would be impossible without a central controlling sun, so harmonious life is impossible without the recognition of Infinite Spirit as that Power, whose generic tendency serves to control each individual being into its proper orbit. This is the teaching of the Bible, and it is also the teaching of the New Thought, which says that life with all its limitless possibilities is a continual outflow from the Infinite which we may turn in any direction that we desire.

But, it may be asked, what happens if we go counter to this generic law of Spirit? This is an important question, and I must leave the answer for further consideration.

IV
Conclusion

I concluded my last chapter with the momentous question, What happens if we go counter to the generic law of Spirit? What happens if we go counter to any natural law? Obviously, the law goes counter to us. We can use the laws of Nature, but we cannot alter them. By opposing any natural law we place ourselves in an inverted position with regard to it, and therefore, viewed from this false standpoint, it appears as though the law itself were working against us with definite purpose. But the inversion proceeds entirely from ourselves, and not from any change in the action of the law. The law of Spirit, like all other natural laws, is in itself impersonal; but we carry into it, so to speak, the reflection of our own personality, though we cannot alter its generic character; and therefore, if we oppose its generic tendency towards the universal good, we shall find in it the reflection of our own opposition and waywardness.

The law of Spirit proceeds unalterably on its course, and what is spoken of in popular phraseology as the Divine wrath is nothing else than the reflex action which naturally follows when we put ourselves in opposition to this law. The evil that results is not a personal intervention of the Universal Spirit, which would imply its entering into specific manifestation, but it is the natural outcome of the causes that we ourselves have set in motion. But the effect to ourselves will be precisely the same as if they were brought about by the volition of an adverse personality, though we may not realize that in truth the personal element is our own. And if we are at all aware of the wonderfully complex nature of man, and the various interweavings of principles which unite the material body at one end of the scale to the purely spiritual Ego at the other, we shall have some faint idea of on how vast a field these adverse influences may operate, not being restricted to the plane of outward manifestation, but acting equally on those inner planes which give rise to the outer and are of a more enduring nature.

Thus the philosophic study of Spirit, so far from affording any excuse for laxity of conduct, adds an emphatic definiteness to the Bible exhortation to flee from the wrath of God. But, on the other hand, it delivers us from groundless terrors, the fear lest our repentance should not be accepted, the fear lest we should be rejected for our inability to subscribe to some traditional dogma, the fear of utter uncertainty regarding the future—fears which make life bitter and the prospect of death appalling to those who are in bondage to them. The knowledge that we are dealing with a power which is no respecter of persons, and in which is no variableness, which is, in fact, an unalterable Law, at once delivers us from all these terrors.

The very unchangeableness of Law makes it certain that no amount of past opposition to it, whether from ignorance or willfulness, will prevent it from working in accordance with its own beneficent and life-giving character as soon as we quit our inverted position and place ourselves in our true relation towards it. The laws of Nature do not harbor revenge; and once we adapt our methods to their character, they will work for us without taking any retrospective notice of our past errors. The law of Spirit may be more complex than that of electricity, because, as expressed in us, it is the law of conscious individuality; but it is none the less a purely natural law, and follows the universal rule, and therefore we may dismiss from our minds, as a baseless figment, the fear of any Divine power treasuring up anger against us on account of bygones, if we are sincerely seeking to do what is right now. The new causes which we put in motion now will produce their proper effect as surely as the old causes did; and thus by inaugurating a new sequence of good we shall cut off the old sequence of evil. Only, of course, we cannot expect to bring about the new sequence while continuing to repeat the old causes, for the fruit must necessarily reproduce the nature of the seed. Thus we are the masters of the situation, and, whether in this world or the next, it rests with ourselves either to perpetuate the evil or to wipe it out and put the good in its place. And it may be noticed in passing that the great central Christian doctrine is based upon the most perfect knowledge of this law, and is the practical application to a profound problem of the deepest psychological science. But this is a large subject, and cannot be suitably dealt with here.

Much has been written and said on the origin of evil, and a volume might be filled with the detailed study of the subject; but for all practical purposes it may be summed up in the one word limitation. For what is the ultimate cause of all strife, whether public or private, but the notion that the supply of good is limited? With the bulk of mankind this is a fixed idea, and they therefore argue that because there is only a certain limited quantity of good, the share in their possession can be increased only by correspondingly diminishing some one else's share. Any one entertaining the same idea, naturally resents the attempt to deprive him of any portion of this limited quantity; and hence arises the whole crop of envy, hatred, fraud, and violence, whether between individuals, classes, or nations. If people only realized the truth that "good" is not a certain limited quantity, but a stream continuously flowing from the exhaustless Infinite, and ready to take any direction we choose to give it, and that each one is able by the action of his own thought to draw from it indefinitely, the substitution of this new and true idea for the old and false one of limitation would at one stroke remove all strife and struggle from the world; every man would find a helper instead of a competitor in every other, and the very laws of Nature, which now so often seem to war against us, would be found a ceaseless source of profit and delight.

"They could not enter into rest because of unbelief," "they limited the Holy One of Israel": in these words the Bible, like the New Thought, traces all the sorrow of the world—that terrible *Weltschmerz* which expresses itself with such direful influence through the pessimistic literature of the day—to the one root of a false belief, the belief in man's limitation. Only substitute for it the true belief, and the evil would be at an end. Now the ground of this true belief is that clear apprehension of "the Father" which, as I have shown, forms the basis of Jesus' teaching. If, from one point of view, the Intelligent Universal Life-Principle is a Power to be obeyed, in the same sense in which we have to obey all the laws of Nature, from the opposite point of view, it is a power to be used. We must never lose sight of the fact that obedience to any natural law in its generic tendency necessarily carries with it a corresponding power of using that law in specific application. This is the old proverb that knowledge is power. It is the old paradox with which Jesus posed the ignorant scribes as to how David's Lord could also be his Son. The word "David" means "Beloved" and to be beloved implies that reciprocal sympathy which is intuitive knowledge. Hence David, the Beloved, is the man who has realized his true relation as a Son to his Father and who is "in tune with the Infinite." On the other hand, this "Infinite" is his "Lord" because it is the complex of all those unchangeable Laws from which it is impossible to swerve without suffering consequent loss of power; and on the other, this knowledge of the innermost principles of All-Being puts him in possession of unlimited powers which he can apply to any specific purpose that he will; and thus he stands towards them in the position of a father who has authority to command the services of his son. Thus David's "Lord," becomes by a natural transition his "Son."

And it is precisely in this that the principle of "Sonship" consists. It is the raising of man from the condition of bondage as a servant by reason of limitation to the status of a son by the entire removal of all limitations. To believe and act on this principle is to "believe on the Son of God," and a practical belief in our own sonship thus sets us free from all evil and from all fear of evil—it brings us out of the kingdom of death into the kingdom of Life. Like everything else, it has to grow, but the good seed of liberating Truth once planted in the heart is sure to germinate, and the more we Endeavour to foster its growth by seeking to grasp with our understanding the reason of these things and to realize our knowledge in practice, the more rapidly we shall find our lives increase in livingness—a joy to ourselves, a brightness to our homes, and a blessing expanding to all around in ever-widening circles.

Enough has now been said to show the identity of principle between the teaching of the Bible and that of the New Thought. Treated in detail, the subject would extend to many volumes explanatory of the Old and New Testaments, and if that great work were ever carried out I have no hesitation in saying that the agreement would be found to extend to the minutest particulars. But the hints contained in the foregoing papers will, I hope, suffice to show that there is nothing antagonistic between the two systems, or, rather, to show that they are one—the statement of the One Truth which always has been and always will be. And if what I have now endeavored to put before my readers should lead any of them to follow up the subject more fully for themselves, I can promise them an inexhaustible store of wonder, delight, and strength in the study of the Old Book in the light of the New Thought.

1902.

Chapter XX

Jachin and Boaz

"And he reared up the pillars before the temple, one on the right hand, and the other on the left; and called the name of that on the right hand Jachin, and the name of that on the left Boaz." (II Chron. iii, 17.)

Very likely some of us have wondered what was the meaning of these two mysterious pillars set up by Solomon in front of his temple, and why they were called by these strange names; and then we have dropped the subject as one of those inexplicable things handed down in the Bible from old time which, we suppose, can have no practical interest for us at the present day. Nevertheless, these strange names are not without a purpose. They contain the key to the entire Bible and to the whole order of Nature, and as emblems of the two great principles that are the pillars of the universe, they fitly stood at the threshold of that temple which was designed to symbolize all the mysteries of Being.

In all the languages of the Semitic stock the letters J and Y are interchangeable, as we see in the modern Arabic "Yakub" for "Jacob" and the old Hebrew "Yaveh" for "Jehovah." This gives us the form "Yachin," which at once reveals the enigma. The word Yak signifies "one"; and the termination "hi," or "him," is an intensitive which may be rendered in English by "only." Thus the word "Jachin" resolves itself into the words "one only," the all-embracing Unity.

The meaning of Boaz is clearly seen in the book of Ruth. There Boaz appears as the kinsman exercising the right of pre-emption so familiar to those versed in Oriental law—a right which has for its purpose the maintenance of the Family as the social unit. According to this widely-spread custom, the purchaser, who is not a member of the family, buys the property subject to the right of kinsmen within certain degrees to purchase it back, and so bring it once more into the family to which it originally belonged. Whatever may be our personal opinions regarding the vexed questions of dogmatic theology, we can all agree as to the general principle indicated in the role acted by Boaz. He brings back the alienated estate into the family—that is to say, he "redeems" it in the legal sense of the word. As a matter of law his power to do this results from his membership in the family; but his motive for doing it is love, his affection for Ruth. Without pushing the analogy too far we may say, then, that Boaz represents the principle of redemption in the widest sense of reclaiming an estate by right of relationship, while the innermost moving power in its recovery is Love.

This is what Boaz stands for in the beautiful story of Ruth, and there is no reason why we should not let the same name stand for the same thing when we seek the meaning of the mysterious pillar. Thus the two pillars typify Unity and the redeeming power of Love, with the significant suggestion that the redemption results from the Unity. They correspond with the two "bonds," or uniting principles spoken of by St. Paul, "the Unity of the Spirit which is the Bond of Peace," and "Love, which is the Bond of Perfectness."

The former is Unity of Being; the latter, Unity of Intention: and the principle of this Dual-Unity is well illustrated by the story of Boaz. The whole story proceeds on the idea of the Family as the social unit, the root-conception of all Oriental law, and if we consider the Family in this light, we shall see how exactly it embodies the two-fold idea of Jachin and Boaz, unity of Being and unity of Thought. The Family forms a unit because all the members proceed from a common progenitor, and are thus all of one blood; but, although this gives them a natural unity of Being of which they cannot divest themselves, it is not enough in itself to make them a united family, as unfortunately experience too often shows. Something more is wanted, and that something is Love. There must be a personal union brought about by sympathetic Thought to complete the natural union resulting from birth. The inherent unity must be expressed by the Individual volition of each member, and thus the Family becomes the ideally perfect social unit; a truth to which St. Paul alludes when he calls God the Father from Whom every family in heaven and on earth is named. Thus Boaz stands for the principle which brings back to the original Unity that which has been for a time separated from it. There has never been any separation of actual Being—the family right always subsisted in the property even while in the hands of strangers, otherwise it could never have been brought back; but it requires the Love principle to put this right into effective operation.

When this begins to work in the knowledge of its right to do so, then there is the return of the individual to the Unity, and the recognition of himself as the particular expression of the Universal in virtue of his own nature.

These two pillars, therefore, stand for the two great spiritual principles that are the basis of all Life: Jachin typifying the Unity resulting from Being, and Boaz typifying the Unity resulting from Love. In this Dual-Unity we find the key to all conceivable involution or evolution of Spirit; and it is therefore not without reason that the record of these two ancient pillars has been preserved in our Scriptures. And finally we may take this as an index to the character of our Scriptures generally. They contain infinite meanings; and often those passages which appear on the surface to be most meaningless will be found to possess the deepest significance. The Book, which we often read so superficially, hides beneath its sometimes seemingly trivial words the secrets of other things. The twin pillars Jachin and Boaz bear witness to this truth. **4**

---

4 The following comment was made by Judge Troward, after the publication of this paper in *Expression*:

"*The Two Pillars* of the Universe are Personality and Mathematics, represented by Boaz and Jachin respectively. This is the broadest simplification to which it is possible to reduce things. Balance consists in preserving the Equilibrium or Alternating Current between these two Principles. Personality is the Absolute Factor. Mathematics are the Relative Factor, for they merely Measure different Rates or Scales. They are absolute in this respect. A particular scale having been selected all its sequences will follow by an inexorable Law of Order and Proportion; but the selection of the scale and the change from one scale to another rests entirely with Personality. What Personality can not do is to make one Scale produce the results of another, but it can set aside one scale and substitute another for it. Hence Personality contains in itself the Universal Scale, or can either accommodate itself to lower rates of motion already established, or can raise them to its own rate of motion. Hence Personality is the grand Ultimate Fact in all things.

"Different personalities should be regarded as different degrees of consciousness. They are different degrees of emergence of The Power that knows Itself."

Chapter XXI
Hephzibah

"Thou shalt no more be termed Forsaken; neither shall thy land any more be termed Desolate; but thou shalt be called Hephzibah, and thy land Beulah: for the Lord delighteth in thee, and thy land shall be married" (Isaiah lxii, 4). The name Hephzibah—or, as it might be written, Hafzbah—conveys a very distinct idea to any one who has lived in the East, and calls up a string of familiar words all containing the same root *hafz*, which signifies "guarding" or "taking care of," such as *hafiz*, a protector, *muhafiz*, a custodian, as in the word *muhafiz daftar*, a head record-keeper; or again, *hifazat*, custody, as *bahifazat polis*, in custody of the police; or again, *daim-ul-hafz*, imprisonment for life, and other similar expressions.

All words from this root suggest the idea of "guarding," and therefore the name Haphzibah at once speaks its own meaning. It is "one who is guarded," a "protected one." And answering to this there must be some power which guards, and the name of this power is given in Hosea ii, 16, where it is called "Ishi." "And it shall be at that day, saith the Lord, that thou shalt call me Ishi; and thou shalt call me no more Baali." "Baali" means "lord," "Ishi" means "husband," and between the two there is a whole world of distinction.

To call the Great Power "Baali" is to live in one world, and to call it "Ishi" is to live in another. The world that is ruled over by Baali is a world of "miserable worms of the dust" and such crawling creatures; but the world that is warmed and lightened by "Ishi" is one in which men and women walk upright, conscious of their own divine nature, instead of dodging about to escape being crushed under the feet of Moloch as he strides through his dominions. If the name Baali did not suggest a wrong idea there would be no need to change it for another, and the change of name therefore indicates the opening of the mind to a larger and sounder conception of the true nature of the Ruling Principle of the universe. It is no imperious autocrat, the very apotheosis of self-glorification, ill-natured and spiteful if its childish vanity be not gratified by hearing its own praises formally proclaimed, often from lips opened only by fear; nor is it an almighty extortioner desiring to deprive us of what we value most, either to satisfy its greed or to demonstrate its sovereignty. This is the image which men make of God and then bow terrified before it, offering a worship which is the worship of Baal, and making life blank because all the livingness has been wiped out of it.

Ishi is the embodiment of the very opposite conception, a wise and affectionate husband, instead of a taskmaster exploiting his slaves. In its true aspect the relation of husband and wife is entirely devoid of any question of relative superiority or inferiority. As well ask whether the front wheel or the back wheel of your bicycle is the more important. The two make a single whole, in which the functions of both parts are reciprocal and equally necessary; yet for this very reason these functions cannot be identical.

In a well-ordered home, where husband and wife are united by mutual love and respect, we see that the man's function is to enter into the larger world and to provide the wife with all that is needed for the maintenance and comfort of the home, while the function of the woman is to be the distributor of what her husband provides, in doing which she follows her own discretion; and a sensible man, knowing that he can trust a sensible wife, does not want to poke his finger into every pie. Thus all things run harmoniously—the woman relieved of responsibilities which are not naturally hers, and the man relieved of responsibilities which are not naturally his. But let any perplexity or danger arise, and the woman knows that from her husband she will receive all the guidance and protection that the occasion may require, he being the wise and strong man that we have supposed him, and having this assurance she is able to pursue the avocations of her own sphere undisturbed by any fears or anxieties.

It is this relation of protection and guidance that is implied by the word Hephzibah. It is the name of those who realize their identity with the all-ordering Divine Spirit. He who realizes this unity with the Spirit finds himself both guided and guarded. And here we touch the fringe of a deep natural mystery, which formed the basis of all that was most valuable in the higher mysteries of the ancients, and the substance of which we must realize if we are to make any progress in the future, whatever form we may adopt to convey the idea to ourselves or others. It is the relation of the individual mind to the Universal Mind, the combination of unity with independence which, though quite clear when we know it by personal experience, is almost inexpressible in words, but which is frequently represented in the Bible under the figure of the marriage relations.

It is a basic principle, and in various modes pervades all Nature, and has been symbolized in every religion the world has known; and in proportion as the individual realizes this relation he will find that he is able to *use* the Universal Mind, while at the same time he is guided and guarded by it. For think what it would be to wield the power of the Universal Mind without having its guidance. It would be the old story of Phaeton trying to drive the chariot of the Sun, which ended in his own destruction; and limitless power without corresponding guidance would be the most terrible curse that any one could bring upon his head.

The relation between the individual mind and the Universal Mind, as portrayed in the reciprocally connected names of Hephzibah and Ishi, must never be lost sight of; for the Great Guiding Mind, immeasurably as it transcends our intellectual consciousness, is not another than *ourselves*. It is The One Self which is the foundation of all the individual selves, and which is, therefore, in all its limitlessness, as entirely one with each individual as though no other being existed. Therefore we do not have to go out of ourselves to find it, for it is the expansion to infinity of all that we truly *are*, having, indeed, no place for those negative forms of evil with which we people a world of illusion, for it is the very Light itself, and in it all illusion is dispelled; but it is the expansion to infinity of all in us that is Affirmative, all that is really living.

Therefore, in looking for its guiding and guarding we are relying upon no borrowed power from *without*, held at the caprice and option of another, but upon the supreme fact of our own nature, which we can use in what direction we will with perfect freedom, knowing no limitation save the obligation not to do violence to our own purest and highest feelings. And this relation is entirely *natural*. We must steer the happy mean between imploring and ignoring. A natural law does not need to be entreated before it will work; and, on the other hand, we cannot make use of it while ignoring its existence.

What we have to do, therefore, is to take the working of the law for granted, and make use of it accordingly; and since that is the law of Mind, and Mind is Personality, this Power, which is at once *ourselves* and above ourselves, may be treated as a Person and may be spoken with, and its replies received by the inner ear of the heart. Any scheme of philosophy that does not result in this personal intercourse with the Divine Mind falls short of the mark. It may be right so far as it goes, but it does not go far enough, and fails to connect us with our vital centre. Names are of small importance so long as the intercourse is real. The Supreme Mind with which we converse is only to be met in the profoundest depths of our own being, and, as Tennyson says, is more perfectly ourselves than our own hands and feet. It is our natural Base; and realizing this we shall find ourselves to be in very truth "guarded ones," guided by the Spirit in all things, nothing too great and nothing too trivial to come within the great Law of our being.

There is another aspect of the Spirit in which it is seen as a Power to be used; and the full flow of life is in the constant alternation between this aspect and the one we have been considering, but always we are linked with the Universal Mind as the flower lives by reason of its root. The connection itself is intrinsic, and can never be severed; but it must be consciously realized before it can be consciously used. All our development consists in the increasing consciousness of this connection, which enables us to apply the higher power to whatever purpose we may have in hand, not merely in the hope that it *may* respond, but with the certain knowledge that by the law of its own nature it is bound to do so, and likewise with the knowledge that by the same law it is bound also to guide us to the selection of right objects and right methods.

Experience will teach us to detect the warning movement of the inner Guide. A deep-seated sense of dissatisfaction, an indescribable feeling that somehow everything is not right, are the indications to which we do well to pay heed; for we are "guarded ones," and these interior monitions are the working of that innermost principle of our own being which is the immediate out flowing of the Great Universal Life into individuality. But, paying heed to this, we shall find ourselves guarded, not as prisoners, but as a loved and honored wife, whose freedom is assured by a protection which will allow no harm to assail her; we shall find that the Law of our nature is Liberty, and that nothing but our own want of understanding can shut us out from it.

Chapter XXII

Mind and Hand

I have before me a curious piece of ancient Egyptian symbolism. It represents the sun sending down to the earth innumerable rays, with the peculiarity that each ray terminates in a hand. This method of representing the sun is so unusual that it suggests the presence in the designer's mind of some idea rather different from those generally associated with the sun as a spiritual emblem; and, if I interpret the symbol rightly, it sets forth the truth, not only of the Divine Being as the Great Source of all Life and of all Illumination, but also the correlative truth of our individual relation to that centre. Each ray is terminated by a hand, and a hand is the emblem of active working; and I think it would be difficult to give a better symbolical representation of innumerable individualities, each working separately, yet all deriving their activity from a common source. The hand is at work upon the earth, and the sun, from which it is a ray, is shining in the heavens; but the connecting line shows whence all the strength and skill of the hand are derived.

If we look at the microcosm of our own person we find this principle exactly reproduced. Our hand is the instrument by which all our work is done—literary, artistic, mechanical, or household—but we know that all this work is really the work of the mind, the will-power at the centre of our system, which first determines what is to be done, and then sets the hand to work to do it; and in the doing of it the mind and hand become one, so that the hand is none other than the mind working. Now, transferring this analogy to the microcosm, we see that we each stand in the same relation to the Universal Mind that our hand does to our individual mind—at least, that is our normal relation; and we shall never put forth our full strength except from this standpoint.

We rightly realize our will as the centre of our individuality, but we should do better to picture our individuality as an ellipse rather than a circle, a figure having two "conjugate foci," two equilibrated centers of revolution rather than a single one, one of which is the will-power or faculty of *doing*, and the other the consciousness or perception of *being*. If we realize only one of these two centers we shall lose both mental and moral balance. If we lose sight of that centre which is our personal will, we shall become flabby visionaries without any backbone; and if, in our anxiety to develop backbone, we lost sight of the other centre, we shall find that we have lost that which corresponds to the lungs and heart in the physical body, and that our backbone, however perfectly developed, is rapidly drying up for want of those functions which minister vitality to the whole system, and is only fit to be hung up in a museum to show what a rigid, lifeless thing the strongest vertebral column becomes when separated from the organization by which alone it can receive nourishment. We must realize the one focus of our individuality as clearly as the other, and bring both into equal balance, if we would develop all our powers and rise to that perfection of Life which has no limits to its glorious possibilities.

Keeping the ancient Egyptian symbol before used, and considering ourselves as the hand, we find that we derive all our power from an infinite centre; and because it is infinite we need never fear that we shall fail to draw to ourselves all that we require for our work, whether it be the intelligence to lay hold of the proper tool, or the strength to use it. And, moreover, we learn from the symbol that this central power is generic. This is a most important truth. It is the centre from which all the hands proceed, and is as fully open to any one hand as to any other. Each hand is doing its separate work, and the whole of the central energy is at its disposal for its own specific purpose. The work of the central energy, as such, is to supply vitality to the hands, and it is they that differentiate this universal power into all the varied forms of application which their different aptitudes and opportunities suggest. We, as the hands, live and work because the Central Mind lives and works in us. We are one with it, and it is one with us; and so long as we keep this primal truth before us, we realize ourselves as beings of unlimited goodness and intelligence and power, and we work in the fullness of strength and confidence accordingly; but if we lose sight of this truth, we shall find that the strongest will must get exhausted at last in the unequal struggle of the individual against the universe.

For if we do not recognize the Central Mind as the source of our vitality, we are literally "fighting for our own hand," and all the other hands are against us, for we have lost the principle of connection with them. This is what must infallibly happen if we rely on nothing but our individual will-power. But if we realize that the will is the power by which we give out, and that every giving out implies a corresponding taking in, then we shall find in the boundless ocean of central living Spirit the source from which we can go on taking in *ad infinitum*, and which thus enables us to give out to any extent we please. But for wise and effective giving out a strong and enlightened will is an absolute necessity, and therefore we do well to cultivate the will, or the active side of our nature. But we must equally cultivate the receptive side also; and when we do this rightly by seeing in the Infinite Mind the one source of supply, our will-power becomes intensified by the knowledge that the whole power of the Infinite is present to back it up; and with this continual sense of Infinite Power behind us we can go calmly and steadily to the accomplishment of any purpose, however difficult, without straining or effort, knowing that it shall be achieved, not by the hand only, but by the invincible Mind that works through it. "Not by might, nor by power, but by My Spirit, saith the Lord of hosts."

1902.

Chapter XXIII

The Central Control

In contemplating the relations between body, soul, and spirit, between Universal Mind and individual mind, the methodized study of which constitutes Mental Science, we must never forget that these relations indicate, not the separateness, but the unity of these principles. We must learn not to attribute one part of our action to one part of our being, and another to another. Neither the action nor the functions are split up into separate parts. The action is a whole, and the being that does it is a whole, and in the healthy organism the reciprocal movements of the principles are so harmonious as never to suggest any feeling than that of a perfectly whole and undivided self. If there is any other feeling we may be sure that there is abnormal action somewhere, and we should set ourselves to discover and remove the cause of it. The reason for this is that in any perfect organism there cannot be more than one centre of control.

A rivalry of controlling principles would be the destruction of the organic wholeness; for either the elements would separate and group themselves round one or other of the centers, according to their respective affinities, and thus form two distinctive individualities, or else they would be reduced to a condition of merely chaotic confusion; in either case the original organism would cease to exist. Seen in this light, therefore, it is a self-evident truth that, if we are to retain our individuality; in other words, if we are to continue to exist, it can be only by retaining our hold upon the central controlling principle in ourselves; and if this be the charter of our being, it follows that all our future development depends on our recognizing and accepting this central controlling principle. To this end, therefore, all our endeavors should be directed; for otherwise all our studies in Mental Science will only lead us into a confused labyrinth of principles and counter-principles, which will be considerably worse than the state of ignorant simplicity from which we started.

This central controlling principle is the Will, and we must never lose sight of the fact that all the other principles about which we have learnt in our studies exist only as its instruments. The Will is the true self, of which they are all functions, and all our progress consists of our increased recognition of the fact. It is the Will that says "I AM"; and therefore, however exalted, or even in their higher developments apparently miraculous, our powers may be, they are all subject to the central controlling power of the Will. When the enlightened Will shall have learnt to identify itself perfectly with the limitless powers of knowledge, judgment, and creative thought which are at its disposal, then the individual will have attained to perfect wholeness, and all limitations will have passed away for ever.

And nothing short of this consciousness of Perfect Wholeness can satisfy us. Everything that falls short of it is in that degree an embodiment of the principle of Death, that great enemy against which the principle of Life must continue to wage unceasing war, in whatever form or measure it may show itself, until "death is swallowed up in victory." There can be no compromise. Either we are affirming Life, as a principle, or we are denying it, no matter on how great or how small a scale; and the criterion by which to determine our attitude is our realization of our own Wholeness. Death is the principle of disintegration; and whenever we admit the power of any portion of our organism, whether spiritual or bodily, to induce any condition *independently of the intention of the Will*, we admit that the force of disintegration is superior to the controlling centre in ourselves, and we conceive of ourselves as held in bondage by an adversary, from which bondage the only way of release is by the attainment of a truer way of thinking.

And the reason is that, either through ignorance or carelessness, we have surrendered our position of control over the system as a whole, and have lost the element of *Purpose*, around which the consciousness of individuality must always centre. Every state of our consciousness, whether active or passive, should be the result of a distinct *purpose* adopted by our own free will; for the passive states should be quite as much under the control of the Will as the active. It is the lack of *purpose* that deprives us of power. The higher and more clearly defined our purpose, the greater stimulus we have for realizing our control over *all* our faculties for its attainment; and since the grandest of all purposes is the strengthening and ennobling of Life, in proportion as we make this our aim we shall find ourselves in union with the Supreme Universal Mind, acting each in our individual sphere for the furtherance of the same purpose which animates the ruling principle of the Great Whole, and, as a consequence, shall find that its intelligence and powers are at our disposal.

But in all this there must be no strain. The true exercise of the Will is not an exercise of unnatural force. It is simply the leading of our powers into their natural channels by intelligently recognizing the direction in which those channels go. However various in detail, they have one clearly defined common tendency towards the increasing of Life—whether in ourselves or in others—and if we keep this steadily in view, all our powers, whether interior or exterior, will be found to work so harmoniously together that there will be no sense of independent action on the part of any one of them. The distinctions drawn for purposes of study will be laid aside, and the Self in us will be found to be the realization of a grand ideal being, at once individual and universal, consciously free in its individual wholeness and in its joyous participation in the Life of the Universal Whole.

Chapter XXIV

What Is Higher Thought?

Resolution passed October, 1902, by the Kensington Higher Thought Centre.

"That the Centre stands for the definite teaching of absolute Oneness of Creator and Creation—Cause and Effect—and that nothing which may contradict or be in opposition to the above principles be admitted to the 'Higher Thought' Centre Platform.

"By Oneness of Cause and Effect is meant, that Effect (man) does consist only of what Cause is; but a part (individual personality) is not therefore co-extensive with the whole."

This Resolution is of the greatest importance. Once admit that there is *any* Power outside yourself, however beneficent you may conceive it to be, and you have sown the seed which must sooner or later bear the fruit of "*Fear*" which is the entire ruin of Life, Love and Liberty. There is no *via media*. Say we are only reflections, however accurate, of The Life, and in the admission we have given away our Birthright. However small or plausible may be the germ of thought which admits that we are anything less in principle than The Life Itself, it must spring up to the ultimate ruin of the Life-Principle itself. We *are* It itself. The difference is only that between the generic and the specific of the *same* thing. We must contend earnestly, both within ourselves and outwardly, for the *one great foundation* and never, now on to all eternity, admit for a single instant any thought which is opposed to this, the Basic Truth of Being.

The leading ideas connected with Higher Thought are (I) That Man controls circumstances, instead of being controlled by them, and (II) as a consequence of the foregoing, that whatever teaches us to *rely* on power *borrowed* from a source *outside* ourselves is *not* Higher Thought; and that whatever explains to us the *Infinite* source of *our own inherent* power and the consequent *limitless* nature of that power *is* Higher Thought. This avoids the use of terms which may only puzzle those not accustomed to abstract phraseology, and is substantially the same as the resolution of October, 1902.

Chapter XXV

Fragments

1. God is Love.
   Man, having the understanding of God, speaks the Word of Power.

2. Man gives utterance to God.

3. The Father is Equilibrium.
   The Son is Concentration of the *same* Spirit.
   The Spirit is Projection.

The Tri-une Relation—always consists of these Three:

(I) The Potential—(II) The Ideal—(III) The Concrete.

(I) The Potential is Life in its most highly abstract mode not yet brought into Form even as Thought. Not particularized in *any* way.

(II) The Ideal is the particularizing of the Potential into a certain Formulated Thought.

(III) The Concrete is the Manifestation of the Formulated Thought in Visible Form.

What everybody wants is to become *more alive*—as Jesus said, "I am come that they might have Life and might have it more abundantly"—and it is only on the basis of realizing ourselves as a *perfect unity throughout*, not made up of opposing parts, and that unity *Spirit*, that we can realize in ourselves the *Livingness* which *Spirit is*, and which we *as Spirit* ought to be.

Hence perfect demonstration.

"The Truth shall make you Free"
Life   :
Love   : = The Truth
Liberty :

The Ultimate Truth will always be found to consist of these three, and anything that is contrary to them is contrary to Fundamental Truth.

WORSHIP

Worship consists in the recognition of the *Personal* Nature of Holy Spirit, and in the Continual Alternation (Pulsation) between the two positions of "I am the Person that Thou art," and "Thou art the Person that I am." The Two Personalities are One.

www.ingramcontent.com/pod-product-compliance
Lightning Source LLC
Chambersburg PA
CBHW020011050426
42450CB00005B/419